# Basketball
## STARTLING STORIES
## BEHIND THE RECORDS

# Basketball
## STARTLING STORIES
## BEHIND THE RECORDS

• • • • • • • • • •

## Jim Benagh

 Sterling Publishing Co., Inc.   New York

## Other Sports Titles by Jim Benagh

Baseball: Startling Stories Behind the Records
Football: Startling Stories Behind the Records

**Library of Congress Cataloging-in-Publication Data**

Benagh, Jim, 1937–
    Basketball : startling stories behind the records / Jim Benagh.
        p.    cm.
    Includes index.
    ISBN 0-8069-7292-0
    1. Basketball—History.   2. Basketball—Records.   I. Title.
    GV883.B46   1991
    796.323—dc20                                          90-22886
                                                               CIP

10  9  8  7  6  5  4  3  2  1

© 1991 by Jim Benagh
Published by Sterling Publishing Company, Inc.
387 Park Avenue South, New York, N.Y. 10016
Distributed in Canada by Sterling Publishing
% Canadian Manda Group, P.O. Box 920, Station U
Toronto, Ontario, Canada M8Z 5P9
Distributed in Great Britain and Europe by Cassell PLC
Villiers House, 41/47 Strand, London WC2N 5JE, England
Distributed in Australia by Capricorn Ltd.
P.O. Box 665, Lane Cove, NSW 2066
*Manufactured in the United States of America*
*All rights reserved*

Sterling ISBN 0-8069-7292-0

# Contents

# • I •

# The Century Club: Basketball's 100-point Scorers

## Bevo, the Player
## Who Saved a College

Whoever initiated the phrase "records are made to be broken" was wrong about the records of Clarence (Bevo) Francis. It has been almost four decades since the gangly Ohio farmboy rose to national fame at a tiny school named Rio Grande College. Yet most of his records, which were astounding in the making, remain with us. Among them:

*Most Points in a Game* (113): Bevo Francis, 1954

*Most Field Goals Attempted, Game* (71): Bevo Francis, 1954

*Most Field Goals Made, Game* (38): Bevo Francis, 1954

*Most Free Throws Attempted, Game* (45): Bevo Francis, 1954

*Most Free Throws Made, Game* (37): Bevo Francis, 1954

*Highest Average per Game* (46.5): Bevo Francis, 1953–54

7

*Most Free Throws Attempted, Season* (510): Bevo Francis, 1953–54

*Most Games over 50 Points, Season* (8): Bevo Francis, 1953–54

*Most Games over 50 Points, Career* (14): Bevo Francis, 1952–54

But the record books tell only part of the story.

Take the last record mentioned above, for instance. Bevo scored over 50 points on 14 occasions, right?

Wrong. Actually, Bevo topped 50 points in 28 games. And his lofty 46.5-point scoring average, which stands out so prominently in current college record books, is also misleading. Bevo may have averaged 46.5 as a sophomore, but he did even better (50.1) playing for the Rio Grande College varsity as a freshman. As for that unbelievable 113-point outburst in a single game, well . . . there was a game the year before when he actually tallied more!

Bevo Francis was almost too much to believe when he arrived at the sleepy little campus (enrollment: 92) in a southern Ohio town by the same name as the college. "Rye-o Grand," the natives pronounced it. Not "Ree-o Grand." Before long, anyone in America who followed the sports pages knew about "Rye-o Grand" and its freshman superstar Bevo Francis. In his freshman year, Francis became the most celebrated athlete in America. The fact that Rio Grande—financially ailing—was on the brink of closing down just added to the Bevo Francis legend.

But Francis' astronomical statistics of that initial season, 1952–53, were brought down to earth by the people entrusted to keep intercollegiate records. Many of the stats were erased because of technicalities. Since college teams could not bring the 6-foot-9 center down to size on the court, they did it through a group of coaches in a committee room.

Rio Grande for years had gone unnoticed playing the same type of schedule—a catch-as-catch-can mixture of small colleges, military bases and junior colleges. But in 1953, after the Redmen, with Bevo, had posted an untarnished 39–0 season and stole national headlines from bigger and better-established universities, little Rio Grande College came under attack. The team's schedule was harshly denounced by the national college coaches' association. A decision was made to rule out many of Bevo's first-year performances—retroactively. All but 12 games would be disallowed by the NCAA's new "interpretation" that statistics would be accepted only in games involving "four-year, degree-granting schools." Wiped out were Bevo's performances against junior colleges, military teams and business schools. Gone were the 116-point performance, the 50-point average and half the games in which Bevo scored 50 or more points. They were victims of committeemen who never saw him play.

Rio Grande's own coach, a chesty outspoken promoter named Newt Oliver, battled hopelessly against the big-time coaches. The coach from Ohio State was one of the leading agitators, having accused Rio Grande of playing a "trumped-up schedule." Oliver offered to book Ohio State for the following season. The Buckeye coach made a hasty retreat.

But even the Ohio State coach was forced to admit publicly, "We have to be a little careful in Ohio about saying anything derogatory about Bevo Francis, who may be a great ballplayer. I say this because he's sort of a common people's All-American."

Indeed he was. A season later, when he was a sophomore, many major universities 50 times Rio Grande's size scheduled games with the Redmen; teams such as North Carolina State, Miami, Providence, Villanova and Wake Forest knew Bevo would build up the gate. Major arena promoters in New York City, Philadelphia, Bos-

*UP AND IN: Nobody in college basketball history scored points like Clarence (Bevo) Francis.*

ton, Indianapolis, St. Louis and Cincinnati beckoned Rio Grande, too.

Bevo did not disappoint his newly found followers. As a sophomore he went out and set his national records all over again. The legend was reborn. Bevo not only scored the most points ever for a single game (113), but the second (84) and third (82) most points, too. Only the major Ohio universities shied away from the little giant-killers from downstate Rio Grande.

Bevo Francis' story is almost Hollywoodish.

Born in 1932, Clarence Francis was an only child. His father, who worked in a brickyard, nicknamed him "Beeve" after a popular soft drink of the era. "Beeve" became "Bevo" after a matter of time. Bevo was a slow starter in sports and his career was further detoured when he transferred from one high school to another, thus being forced to sit out a season at Wellsville (Ohio) High.

Bevo finally got to play as a high-school junior, but he would be ineligible again as a senior because he would be too old (at 20) under the state rules. Bevo made the best of his single year of varsity competition, though. Playing for ex-Rio Grande star Newt Oliver, who was coaching at Wellsville at the time, Francis averaged 31 points a game and led the team to a 19–1 record.

After this fine year at the high school, Newt Oliver made a bid for the coaching job at his alma mater. He was willing to overlook Rio Grande College's weaknesses (a 150-seat gym, a $3,500 annual salary, and a school on the verge of going under) if Rio Grande would overlook his obstacles (he was only 27, with but three years of high-school coaching behind him). Oliver got the job— and with it an unheated office, a showerless locker room and one basketball. Appropriately, the ball was lopsided.

Fast-talking Oliver, however, convinced a wealthy Rio Grande alumnus to provide a $3,000 contribution for the scholarship fund. That helped the coach bring in his protege, Bevo Francis, from Wellsville. Over 60 other schools wanted Bevo, but Oliver was forever the supersalesman.

Oliver got some other players, too. His recruiting pitch and his preseason pep talk emphasized one point: "Some day we will be playing in Madison Square Garden." He got good players all right, but one of them once remarked at a team meeting, "Coach, the only garden we will see is one with a hoe."

The players sold Oliver short. But they were willing to help him attain two goals that he felt would put the college on the map; one was to average 100 points a game as a team, something that had never been done at the college level, and the other was to have Bevo average 50 points, another out-of-sight figure. Together with winning, Oliver felt, these feats would get Rio Grande recognition. Oliver's first contribution toward Rio's betterment was to double the schedule to 39 games. With a team that wasn't about to make an instant splash at the box office and a 150-seat home court, Rio Grande could use all the first-year income it could get.

Rio Grande opened its 1952–53 season officially with Cumberland College, a school with an enrollment 18 times larger. Bevo was unspectacular in his debut, but he scored 45 as the Redmen won handily. Nobody seemed to mind the fact that technically Bevo was finishing his high-school curriculum at the same time he was taking college courses. The Rio Grande president had cleared that matter up rather easily with the Ohio college athletic association.

The opening night "crowd" was 100. The attendance was up to 110 for the next game against Sue Bennett College, which was treated to a 58-point attack by the star center. Gradually Bevo began raising his point score to 69, then 72, then 76 as the season wore on. Then in game No. 18, Bevo pumped in a national record—116 points—against Ashland Junior College of Kentucky. Bevo, his 20-foot jump shot on target and his hook shots flawless, made 47 field goals that night. A full house of 150 cheered him on at Community Hall. Gone would be the days when Rio Grande would draw 62 fans and a paid gate of $19.20, as had happened once early in the season.

Bevo's fluctuating point-average stayed over 50 after that night. In fact, when the statisticians compiled their final figures, they learned that against Ashland Bevo had scored 55 points in the last 10-minute quarter alone.

The 116 points surpassed the collegiate record of 87, set—ironically—by a former Rio Grande star. The major-college best at the time was 85, by All-American Paul Arizin of Villanova. Most record books recognized Arizin's feat, though interestingly enough it was *not* against a four-year, degree-granting institution.

Rio Grande was so far out of the mainstream of national interest at the time that no one bothered to keep track of Bevo's field-goal attempts against Ashland. Oliver has recalled that he took about 60 to 70. But no one had come close to 47 field goals made, regardless of the level of competition. If there were any critics of the Rio Grande schedule at that juncture, they had not made themselves heard.

In three successive games after that Ashland game on January 9, Bevo scored 63, 55 and 51 points. The national recognition was beginning. A New York City paper dispatched a man to Rio Grande and Bevo treated him to a series of great games. Finishing the season in a flurry, Bevo totaled 1924 points. The current NCAA record is 1329 by Earl (The Pearl) Monroe.

Now Rio Grande was in demand for the 1953–54 season, despite the statistical putdown by the NCAA. A college that began the season with $35 guarantees for away games was turning down offers in the low five figures. The Redmen earned $25,000 for Dayton's March of Dimes Fund alone, and received a handsome payday of their own. No longer would the wives of Bevo Francis and Newt Oliver have to throw the team's uniforms in the wash with their own family laundry. No longer would there be a shortage of basketballs for practice. And no longer would the Redmen have to perform at the 150-seat "Hog Pen." All 1953–54 games would be on the road. The basketball team was paying off the school debts and attracting new students at the same time.

While Rio Grande College basked in its newfound glory and people like gubernatorial candidate Jim Rhodes were seeking Bevo's endorsement, the major-college coaches were meeting in Kansas City to destroy his achievements. Soon his records were watered down, and within Ohio an athletic board ordered Rio Grande to cut its next schedule down to 25 regular-season games.

At the same time, *Life*, *Look*, *True*, *Newsweek*, *Sport*, and *Time* magazines and scores of major newspapers were dropping in to chronicle the legend. The nation was trying to erase the memory of recent and widespread basketball betting scandals. Bevo, trying to struggle on limited expense money, was untouched. In fact, he had become a public official himself, winning the constable election of Raccoon Township.

Rio Grande College, buoyed by its basketball success, looked forward to the new school year. The team was happy, too, as it was assured of a sellout opener in Buffalo, New York. Some 5,000 fans paid to watch Bevo score 64 points—against a four-year, degree-granting school.

Next, 13,000 fans were drawn into Madison Square Garden in New York for Bevo's debut there. Unfortunately, Bevo and Rio Grande were at a low ebb. Bevo got 32 but was not impressive, and the Rio Grande winning streak was halted after 40 triumphs. But Bevo came back strong the following night to score 39 against Villanova, a major-college team, in Philadelphia. The Redmen lost by only one point, and critics took a backseat that night. Strengthened by that game, Rio Grande managed to upset some major powers—Providence, Miami, Wake Forest, Butler and Creighton, all away from home. Meanwhile, Bevo was out to reclaim some of the records that were taken away from him. He scored 82 points against Bluffton College, then 84 against Alliance. Crowds were shoehorned into major arenas wherever he played. In Miami, scalpers asked $25 for tickets.

The games against big-time teams made Bevo a more polished player for his contests against the smaller schools. One of the earlier games in 1953–54 was against a small Michigan school named Hillsdale. The Redmen beat them routinely, 82–45, with Bevo garnering 43 himself. A second game—Rio Grande's twentieth contest of the year—was set for Jackson, Ohio, on February 2, 1954. Hillsdale had attempted a slowdown game the first time around, and all scouting reports indicated that the same strategy would be in effect. Hillsdale had about three starters in the 6-foot-5 range and they again would encircle Bevo.

But after the tipoff of the second game, the Redmen ran up several points, pressing and fastbreaking their opponent. Hillsdale could not afford to lay back if it wanted to win. It was the opportunity Bevo needed.

By halftime, he had matched the 43 points scored against Hillsdale in the entire earlier part of the game. With another half like that, he could challenge the collegiate record of 87. Oliver ordered the team to feed him. By the end of the third period, Bevo was up to 74 and going strong. He decided to shoot for 100—something no collegian or pro had ever done, except for his own aborted 116.

He needed 26. He got 39. In all, he wound up with 113

against an official four-year school. No one could take that record away. And nobody has come close to matching it since. While Bevo was making history, the rest of the Rio Grande team combined was scoring a total of 21 points. The final score was, 134–91.

Analyzing the remarkable performance, statisticians credited Bevo with 38 field goals (a record) and a sensational night foul shooting with 37 for 42 (both records).

Just how good was his performance? In another year, college basketball officials would pass a rule that would give the free-throw shooter a "bonus" if he made his first attempt on a one-shot free throw. When Bevo played, he got only one shot—period—unless he was in the act of shooting a field goal. Thus many teams devised the strategy of fouling him as soon as he got the ball; that way he would get one shot. One team fouled him 14 straight times. Had the future rule been in effect on February 2, 1954, Bevo conceivably could have had about 20 more attempts at the foul line and wound up with 130 or so points, not 113!

The record stands. It will be difficult to break under any normal circumstances.

Bevo followed up the Hillsdale game with three straight games in the high 50's, then injured an ankle that left him limping through most of his remaining games. Still, Rio Grande College was 21–7 and Bevo reclaimed all of his records.

With the new foul rule going into effect, and additional experience gained after a hard season, it is fair to theorize that Bevo might have gone on to average 60 points over his final two years and put basketball records out of reach forever. He still had two years of eligibility left. But he dropped out of school to capitalize on his national reputation. He signed to play with a team that toured with the Harlem Globetrotters and later bounced

## 1952–53 Season

| RIO | | OPP. | SITE | BEVO'S PTS. |
|---|---|---|---|---|
| 116 | Rio Grande Alumni | 48 | Community Hall | 44 |
| 84 | Cumberland | 75 | Community Hall | 45 |
| 121 | Sue Bennett | 99 | Community Hall | 58 |
| 108 | Waynesburg | 70 | Community Hall | 46 |
| 93 | Dayton Freshmen | 89 | Community Hall | 35 |
| 111 | Wilberforce | 71 | Community Hall | 69 |
| 93 | Bluefield | 63 | Bluefield, Va. | 21 |
| 88 | Dennison | 78 | Granville, O. | 26 |
| 76 | Marietta | 73 | Marietta, O. | 37 |
| 90 | Beckley | 71 | Beckley, W. Va. | 46 |
| 105 | California State | 73 | Community Hall  . | 72 |
| 114 | Sue Bennett | 68 | London, Ky. | 59 |
| 107 | Steubenville | 58 | Community Hall | 50 |
| 72 | Pikeville | 52 | Pikeville, Ky. | 25 |
| 102 | Lees College | 64 | Jackson, Ky. | 76 |
| 78 | Cumberland | 49 | Williamsburg, Ky. | 34 |
| 91 | Findlay | 88 | Findlay, O. | 44 |
| 150 | Ashland Jr. College | 85 | Community Hall | 116 |
| 119 | Mayo State | 91 | Paintsville, Ky. | 63 |
| 113 | Wright Patterson | 85 | Gallipolis, O. | 55 |
| 101 | Bliss | 53 | Columbus, O. | 51 |
| 84 | Lockbourne Air Force | 50 | Groveport, O. | 36 |
| 66 | Cedarville | 29 | Troy, O. | 38 |
| 79 | Cincinnati Seminary | 54 | Dayton, O. | 42 |
| 133 | Mountain State | 83 | Zanesville, O. | 66 |
| 102 | Beckley | 69 | Huntington, W. Va. | 46 |
| 78 | Steubenville | 65 | Toronto, O. | 41 |
| 97 | Pikeville | 62 | Wellsville, O. | 61 |
| 126 | Mayo State | 98 | Middleport, O. | 60 |
| 104 | Cedarville | 48 | Springfield, O. | 51 |
| 116 | Mountain State | 65 | Parkersburg, W. Va. | 37 |
| 105 | Bliss | 69 | Wellston, O. | 49 |
| 95 | Lockbourne Air Force | 80 | Portsmouth, O. | 47 |
| 128 | Lees College | 57 | Chillicothe, O. | 63 |
| 100 | Wilberforce | 51 | Cincinnati, O. | 52 |
| 128 | Bluefield | 73 | Community Hall | 53 |
| 70 | Ashland Jr. College | 63 | Ashland, Ky. | 25 |
| 111 | Cincinnati Seminary | 86 | Gallipolis, O. | 59 |
| 109 | Wilberforce | 55 | Cleveland, O. | 54 |

| RIO | | OPP. | SITE | BEVO'S PTS. |
|---|---|---|---|---|
| 120 | Erie Tech | 59 | Buffalo, N.Y. | 64 |
| 76 | Adelphi | 83 | New York City | 32 |
| 92 | Villanova | 93 | Philadelphia | 39 |
| 89 | Providence | 87 | Boston, Mass. | 41 |
| 116 | Bluffton | 71 | Bluffton, O. | 82 |
| 82 | Hillsdale | 45 | Hillsdale, Mich. | 43 |
| 98 | Miami | 88 | Miami, Fla. | 48 |
| 77 | North Carolina State | 92 | Raleigh, N.C. | 34 |
| 67 | Wake Forest | 65 | Raleigh, N.C. | 32 |
| 96 | Salem | 99 | Clarksburg, W. Va. | 38 |
| 81 | Butler | 68 | Indianapolis | 48 |
| 86 | Morris Harvey | 63 | Charleston, W. Va. | 41 |
| 107 | Alliance College | 77 | Erie, Pa. | 61 |
| 133 | Alliance College | 68 | Wellsville, O. | 84 |
| 117 | Ashland College | 74 | Gallipolis, O. | 55 |
| 74 | Findlay | 71 | Dayton, O. | 32 |
| 96 | Creighton | 90 | Troy, O. | 49 |
| 74 | Morris Harvey | 62 | Cincinnati | 26 |
| 81 | Buffalo State | 65 | Buffalo, N.Y. | 31 |
| 134 | Hillsdale | 91 | Jackson, O. | 113 |
| 101 | Anderson | 85 | Anderson, Ind. | 59 |
| 115 | Salem | 76 | Huntington, W. Va. | 58 |
| 121 | Ashland | 61 | Ashland, O. | 53 |
| 90 | Arizona State | 74 | Kansas City, Mo. | 28 |
| 65 | S.E. Louisiana | 78 | Kansas City, Mo. | 27 |
| 72 | Shurtleff | 77 | St. Louis, Mo. | 37 |
| 50 | Rockhurst | 56 | Kansas City, Mo. | 22 |
| 75 | Creighton | 93 | Omaha, Neb. | 41 |

## THE 116-POINT GAME

### Rio Grande College

|            | FG | FT | FA | PF | TP  |
|------------|----|----|----|----|-----|
| Francis, c | 47 | 22 | 29 | 1  | 116 |
| Barr, f    | 2  | 0  | 2  | 5  | 4   |
| Moses, f   | 5  | 2  | 3  | 3  | 12  |
| Wiseman, g | 0  | 3  | 5  | 3  | 3   |
| Ripperger, g | 3 | 2 | 2  | 5  | 8   |
| Gossett, f | 1  | 2  | 6  | 5  | 4   |
| Viscoglosi, f | 1 | 1 | 3 | 5  | 3   |
| Davis, g   |    |    |    |    |     |
| Frasher, g |    |    |    |    |     |
| Miller, g  |    |    |    |    |     |
| Totals     | 59 | 32 | 50 | 27 | 150 |

### Ashland Junior College

|            | FG | FT | FA | PF | TP |
|------------|----|----|----|----|----|
| Hobbs, f   | 9  | 5  | 12 | 4  | 23 |
| Kennedy, f | 3  | 3  | 3  | 4  | 9  |
| Dingess, c | 3  | 1  | 1  | 3  | 7  |
| Carr, g    | 0  | 1  | 1  | 5  | 1  |
| Miller, g  | 5  | 6  | 7  | 3  | 16 |
| Slater, f  | 6  | 7  | 13 | 5  | 19 |
| Burgess, f | 2  | 4  | 9  | 3  | 8  |
| Oney, c    | 0  | 2  | 2  | 2  | 2  |
| Totals     | 28 | 29 | 48 | 29 | 85 |

### Quarter Scores

|                       | 1  | 2  | 3  | 4  |
|-----------------------|----|----|----|----|
| Rio Grande College    | 40 | 28 | 27 | 55 |
| Ashland Jr. College   | 20 | 18 | 18 | 29 |

| Rio Grande | | | | Hillsdale | | |
|---|---|---|---|---|---|---|
| | G | F | T | | G | F | T |
| Wiseman | 1 | 2 | 4 | Lowry | 4 | 1 | 9 |
| Barr | 1 | 0 | 2 | Helsted | 6 | 7 | 19 |
| Ripperger | 2 | 5 | 9 | Kincannon | 0 | 3 | 3 |
| Francis | 38 | 37 | 113 | Wagner | 1 | 0 | 2 |
| McKenzie | 0 | 0 | 0 | Davis | 7 | 11 | 25 |
| Vyhnalek | 0 | 0 | 0 | Sewell | 0 | 3 | 3 |
| Moses | 1 | 0 | 2 | Fake | 0 | 2 | 2 |
| Gossett | 0 | 1 | 1 | Neff | 4 | 4 | 12 |
| Weiher | 1 | 0 | 2 | Check | 1 | 1 | 3 |
| Myers | 0 | 1 | 1 | Allinder | 1 | 2 | 4 |
| | | | | Thiendeck | 1 | 0 | 2 |
| | | | | Vushan | 2 | 0 | 4 |
| | | | | Tallmen | 1 | 1 | 3 |
| Totals | 44 | 46 | 134 | Totals | 28 | 35 | 91 |

around the minor leagues. Then he dropped back into the obscurity from which he came.

But he was a legend at a time when a school—and basketball in general—needed help. In his final season, Rio Grande College played before 164,000 fans and got a nice slice of the gate receipts. The school is still in business today, a testimonial to a high-scoring basketball player's talents. He literally saved a college from extinction, which is an incredible feat in itself.

# The Other Collegiate 100-Pointer

A call in 1989 to the National Basketball Association office in New York City to check on the whereabouts of Frank Selvy, who spent a decade in the league, was fruitless.

"Check with the Players Association," the secretary suggested.

But that proved to no avail.

"Check with the Lakers," the Players union suggested.

And did the Los Angeles Lakers know?

"Frank who? Can you spell the last name? Never heard of him."

But surely someone in the Lakers' office must have known of Frank Selvy, who averaged 19 points a game as a rookie for the St. Louis Hawks and later was a prime playmaker for the Laker teams that featured Elgin Baylor and Jerry West.

Finally someone in the executive office had an answer.

"Mr. West said he is living in Greenville, S.C.," said a voice on the other end of the phone.

Frank Who?

In the 1950s, an era when no major college player had yet averaged 30 points a game, every basketball fan knew who Frank Selvy was. Playing for Furman University, Selvy averaged 24.6 points as a sophomore and led the country with 29.5 as a junior.

In midseason of his senior season, 1953–54, he was scoring close to 40 points a game and was on his way to shattering 24 one-season and career records of the National Collegiate Athletic Association (NCAA). He had scored 50 or more points in four games and, like Bevo Francis, he was the focal point of the national media.

Needless to say, the basketball fans in Greenville,

where Furman is located, and his teammates, who shared the national spotlight with him, appreciated the Corbin, Kentucky native.

So did the fans from Corbin. On February 13, 1954, more than 100 of them formed a motorcade to travel 250 miles to Greenville to attend a special "Frank Selvy Night."

Though the nation was still in awe of the 113 points that Bevo Francis had scored just 11 nights before in small-college competition, there was still enough attention for Selvy. In fact, *Life* magazine was preparing a story about Selvy.

It was a special game for South Carolinians, too, because it was the first sports event in the state to be televised live.

Furman's opponent was Newberry College, a small Lutheran school with about 400 male students.

"Just a regular game for us," recalled Selvy, who now makes his home near Greenville, where he represents a paper company.

He said he felt loose in the warmups before the game, and that "I felt like I would have a good night."

It did not turn out to be a regular game or just a good night, however. In the first quarter, Selvy himself outscored the Newberry team, 24–19. By halftime, Selvy had attempted 24 shots and already scored 37 points, close to his full-game average. Furman was winning in a runaway, 77–44. The fans from Corbin combined with the local followers to make the Furman gym come alive.

Meanwhile, at halftime, Selvy recalled: "My teammates got together and decided I'd take all the shots in the second half. The only thing is, they didn't tell me."

It didn't take Selvy long to learn what was going on.

"I figured it out right away, because every time I passed the ball, I'd get it right back."

Selvy began piling up the points. As usual, he took the ball down the court as the team's tall guard— 6-feet-3½ was pretty big in those days—and then he would roam into the center, looking for jumpshots and layups.

In the third quarter he added 25 more points, bringing his game total to 62, a point short of his personal high for a full game.

He also was in range of the NCAA one-game record of 73 points, set by Bill Mlkvy of Temple a couple of years before.

Selvy's teammates had now developed another ploy, and Selvy was going along with it.

"After a while, we were so far ahead, we just let them shoot and got the ball back quickly," Selvy remembered. "We had to keep the Newberry players happy, too. Plus, their coach was good about it. He didn't have his team hold the ball."

In the final quarter, Selvy was putting up everything. He easily passed Mlkvy's record and suddenly was on the brink of scoring 100 points, even if it meant getting 38 points in the final 10-minute quarter. (This was the era before college teams began playing two 20-minute halves.)

With 30 seconds left, Selvy had 94 points, and he quickly made two more field goals. Then with time running out, he made his biggest blunder of the game. On an out-of-bounds play, he mistakenly took the ball to make an in-bound pass as he often did on a normal night.

But a teammate quickly covered for him and got the ball right back to him.

"I took about four or five steps over the midcourt line and let it fly," recalled Selvy. "A jumpshot. There were two seconds left on the clock. There was no way I could really make that shot. I threw the ball and it just happened to go in."

| FURMAN (149) | FG | FT-FTA | PF | TP |
|---|---|---|---|---|
| Bennett, f | 0 | 1–1 | 3 | 1 |
| Floyd, f | 12 | 1–1 | 0 | 25 |
| Fraley, f | 3 | 0–2 | 2 | 6 |
| Poole, f | 0 | 0–0 | 1 | 0 |
| Thomas, c | 5 | 1–1 | 1 | 11 |
| Kyber, c | 0 | 0–2 | 4 | 0 |
| Ruth, c | 0 | 0–0 | 1 | 0 |
| Gordon, c | 0 | 0–0 | 1 | 0 |
| Selvy, g | 41 | 18–22 | 4 | 100 |
| Deardorff, g | 1 | 1–1 | 3 | 3 |
| Wright, g | 0 | 0–0 | 1 | 0 |
| Jones, g | 0 | 1–1 | 2 | 1 |
| Gilreath, g | 1 | 0–0 | 1 | 2 |
| Totals | 63 | 23–31 | 24 | 149 |

| Newberry (95) | FG | FT-FTA | PF | TP |
|---|---|---|---|---|
| Boland, f | 0 | 0–0 | 0 | 0 |
| Warner, f | 2 | 0–4 | 5 | 4 |
| Leitner, f | 6 | 4–7 | 1 | 16 |
| Bailey, f | 0 | 1–5 | 5 | 1 |
| Blanko, c | 14 | 7–10 | 2 | 35 |
| Cone, c | 1 | 0–0 | 2 | 2 |
| Roth, g | 0 | 3–7 | 5 | 3 |
| McElven, g | 1 | 0–0 | 0 | 2 |
| Davis, g | 13 | 6–10 | 2 | 32 |
| Totals | 37 | 21–43 | 22 | 95 |

| By Quarters | 1 | 2 | 3 | 4 | |
|---|---|---|---|---|---|
| Furman | 38 | 39 | 32 | 40— | 149 |
| Newberry | 19 | 25 | 22 | 29— | 95 |

**SELVY'S GAME**
**Quarter by Quarter**

| Q | FGA | FGM | FTA | FTM | Pts. |
|---|---|---|---|---|---|
| 1 | 13 | 10 | 4 | 4 | 24 |
| 2 | 11 | 5 | 5 | 3 | 13 |
| 3 | 15 | 10 | 6 | 5 | 25 |
| 4 | 27 | 16 | 7 | 6 | 38 |
| Totals | 66 | 41 | 22 | 18 | 100 |

The Furman gym was in bedlam. Selvy had scored an even 100 points.

That night, he was given credit for 72 shots and made 41—both major college records. He was 16 for 27 in the final quarter alone. From the foul line, he made 18 of 22 attempts.

Even his Furman teammates had a good night, scoring 49 points among them as Furman won 149–95.

Since then, no major college player has come within 19 points of his record, and only Pete Maravich of Louisiana State has averaged more points in a season than the 41.7 Selvy finished with in 1953-54.

But to this day, he is surprised with his 100.

"I didn't think anybody could score that much," he said. "I still have the videotape from that game, and when I look at it, it seems like I scored about 35 points."

# Wilt's 100-Pointer Got a Bad Press

Early in his major-league basketball career, Wilt Chamberlain commented to a reporter, "Nobody roots for Goliath." The enigmatic behemoth was, of course, his own case in point. Chamberlain's critics probably outnumber his fans. Opposing coaches and players try to cut him down to size with words. Even those who build him up sometimes do it maliciously; a Philadelphia newspaper used to have a standard copydesk rule that Wilt would be listed as 7-feet-3, no matter how many times he insisted he was only 7-feet-1⅜.

For one game in his career, it seemed that no one could fault the most prolific scorer in professional basketball history. It came in 1962, when Chamberlain was ripping apart the National Basketball Association record books with his 50-point scoring bursts—and his 50.4-point average. In the course of the 1961–62 season, when he was playing with the Philadelphia Warriors, Chamberlain twice broke Elgin Baylor's NBA one-game record of 71 points. In December of that season, Wilt tallied 78 points against Baylor's own team, the Los Angeles Lakers, but again the press downgraded Wilt's performance because the game went into three overtimes. About five weeks later, Wilt scored 73 in regulation time. The complaint counter remained closed that day.

Then, late in the season, the Warriors and the New York Knicks—two teams going nowhere—met for a March 2 game. The site of the game seemed like the middle of nowhere, too—Hershey, Pa. For a man enjoying the most spectacular scoring spree in professional basketball history, the Knicks were an inviting opponent. Eight times in games with the Knicks that season, more than against any other team, Wilt got at least 50 points. For the March 2 encounter, it was announced that

*THE CENTURY MARK: Wilt Chamberlain was always a scoring machine, but on March 2, 1962, he even exceeded everyone's expectations.*

# CHAMBERLAIN'S 100-POINT GAME

## Philadelphia (169)

| PLAYER | POS. | MIN. | FGA | FGM | FTA | FTM | REB. | AST. | PF. | PTS. |
|---|---|---|---|---|---|---|---|---|---|---|
| Arizin | F | 31 | 18 | 7 | 2 | 2 | 5 | 4 | 0 | 16 |
| Conlin | | 14 | 4 | 0 | 0 | 0 | 4 | 1 | 1 | 0 |
| Ruklik | | 8 | 1 | 0 | 2 | 0 | 2 | 1 | 2 | 0 |
| Meschery | F | 40 | 12 | 7 | 2 | 2 | 7 | 3 | 4 | 16 |
| Luckenbill | | 3 | 0 | 0 | 0 | 0 | 1 | 0 | 2 | 0 |
| Chamberlain | C | 48 | 63 | 36 | 32 | 28 | 25 | 2 | 2 | 100 |
| Rodgers | G | 48 | 4 | 1 | 12 | 9 | 7 | 20 | 5 | 11 |
| Attles | G | 34 | 8 | 8 | 1 | 1 | 5 | 6 | 4 | 17 |
| Larese | G | 14 | 5 | 4 | 1 | 1 | 1 | 2 | 5 | 9 |
| Totals | | 240 | 115 | 63 | 52 | 43 | 60 | 39 | 25 | 169 |

## New York (147)

| PLAYER | POS. | MIN. | FGA | FGM | FTA | FTM | REB. | AST. | PF. | PTS. |
|---|---|---|---|---|---|---|---|---|---|---|
| Naulls | F | 43 | 22 | 9 | 15 | 13 | 7 | 2 | 5 | 31 |
| Green | F | 21 | 7 | 3 | 0 | 0 | 7 | 1 | 5 | 6 |
| Buckner | | 33 | 26 | 16 | 1 | 1 | 8 | 0 | 4 | 33 |
| Imhoff | C | 20 | 7 | 3 | 1 | 1 | 6 | 0 | 6 | 7 |
| Budd | | 27 | 8 | 6 | 1 | 1 | 10 | 1 | 1 | 13 |
| Guerin | G | 46 | 29 | 13 | 17 | 13 | 8 | 6 | 5 | 39 |
| Butler | G | 32 | 13 | 4 | 0 | 0 | 7 | 3 | 1 | 8 |
| Butcher | | 18 | 6 | 3 | 6 | 4 | 3 | 4 | 5 | 10 |
| Totals | | 240 | 118 | 57 | 41 | 33 | 60 | 17 | 32 | 147 |

**Score by Periods:**

| | 1st | 2nd | 3rd | 4th | Total |
|---|---|---|---|---|---|
| Philadelphia | 42 | 37 | 46 | 44 | 169 |
| New York | 26 | 42 | 38 | 41 | 147 |

## Chamberlain's Scoring by Quarters

| Q | MIN. | FGA | FGM | FTA | FTM | REB. | AST. | PF. | PTS. |
|---|---|---|---|---|---|---|---|---|---|
| 1 | 12 | 14 | 7 | 9 | 9 | 10 | 0 | 0 | 23 |
| 2 | 12 | 12 | 7 | 5 | 4 | 4 | 1 | 1 | 18 |
| 3 | 12 | 16 | 10 | 8 | 8 | 6 | 1 | 0 | 28 |
| 4 | 12 | 21 | 12 | 10 | 7 | 5 | 0 | 1 | 31 |
| Totals | 48 | 63 | 36 | 32 | 28 | 25 | 2 | 2 | 100 |

the Knicks' lone backup center would not be available and an inexperienced rookie, Cleveland Buckner, would have to bolster the pivot position behind the Knicks' regular center Darrell Imhoff.

The Knicks were a terrible team that season. That was taken for granted. And Wilt had the feeling that he was in for a big night at Hershey. A quick opening burst against the Knicks, including a rare perfect showing at the foul line, lifted Wilt's hopes. At the end of the first period, he already had 23 points, almost half a night's work. In the second period he added 18 more.

Meanwhile, Imhoff, a player who earned his reputation for defense, was having his own troubles in the fouling department. He may have been big and strong, but Wilt was just bigger and stronger.

Wilt, blessed by a fine feeder in guard Guy Rodgers, was having a field day at the expense of the hapless Knicks. By the end of the third period, it was obvious he was going to smash his own pro scoring record for one game; he already had 69 points. The fans at Hershey—and there were only about 4,000 of them—began chanting, "Give it to Wilt." Guy Rodgers and the rest of the Warriors obliged. In fact, playmaker Rodgers was so generous he would end up with an even 20 assists.

Chamberlain was having an easy time with the Knicks defense, but then Imhoff fouled out early in the final period. The untried Buckner was summoned into the game. Nobody envied his defensive assignment. Buckner was only 6-foot-9.

Defensively, Wilt paid little attention to Buckner, who was allowed to have a career high 33 points that night. The focus was on offense and just how high Wilt could push his own one-game high. But as Wilt zeroed in on 100, the Knicks began playing a careful and dullish game which enraged the fans who were cheering Wilt on. Fortunately, Warrior coach Frank McGuire remedied the situation by having his players foul the New Yorkers whenever they stalled.

Wilt went back to reaching for 100. He got his 95th point on one of his patented dunk shots, and his 96th on another foul shot. He made his 98th on a dunk. Then he had 1:17 minutes to make two more points.

He shot and missed. He shot again and missed. Time was running out, but Wilt finally put the ball up with 42 seconds left.

He had his 100th point and a fistful of other records.

In a single game, he had shot more times and connected more often from the field than any man in history. More surprisingly, the man who would finish his NBA career with horrendous 51.1 per cent "accuracy" from the free-throw line would this night make 28 of 32—both records that still stand.

One hundred points is not a very vulnerable mark in a league that now stresses defense and balanced teamwork. And even with a lot of teamwork, such as Guy Rodgers displayed that March night in 1962, the record is not likely to be seriously challenged unless a new Wilt Chamberlain comes along.

But there were those who turned their backs on Wilt the night he hit the century mark. They included all-time great Bob Cousy, who said there had been nothing at stake, the Knicks weren't trying and that it was a meaningless late-season game. Who cared? Only history.

# The Night Heater Got Hot

It was January 1960 when the coach of little Burnsville High School in West Virginia decided to go against his principles to help his star player. Jack Stalnaker took the advice of a fellow coach to let Danny Heater, his unselfish star senior, roll up the points in order to draw the attention of college recruiters, who seemed to be bypassing the central West Virginia community.

Heater did the impossible in a January 26 game, scoring 135 points for a national high school record.

But the coach's grand plan almost fell through when he called the closest newspaper, The Clarksburg Exponent.

A harried reporter at the other end of the phone was taking scores and told the coach, "Give me the Burnsville scoring first."

Stalnaker began to say, "Heater, 53 field goals, 29 free throws, 135 points" when the reporter interrupted, "No, not the team scoring, the individual scoring."

Stalnaker tried to explain, but the reporter began to get angry and said not to get smart. The sports editor overheard the conversation and stepped in. It took some time for Stalnaker to convince him that he was for real, not a prankster.

The story not only went out to Clarksburg area readers, but also made the national wires—and Heater began getting inquiries from colleges.

If the newspaper was hesitant, no wonder. After all, it was an improbable performance, something no collegian or pro—much less a schoolboy—had ever accomplished.

It also was improbable that Danny Heater would be the player to do it. Somewhat frail at a shade under 6 feet and 140 pounds, the son of a poor coal-mining family, Heater nevertheless was a standout on the basketball court. He started during all four years at Burnsville

High. Despite his size, he shouldered a big burden: He played center on defense because of his unusual jumping ability.

Heater had helped lead the Bruins to 18 straight victories going into a January 26 game against nearby Widen in the small, archaic Burnsville gym. That season, when Burnsville had a rough game, Heater would come through with 30 or 40 points a game. When the team, which was averaging nearly 100 points a game, had a runaway, Heater was good for less than 10.

Stalnaker was sold on Heater's potential as a collegian, though, and wanted the recruiters to know it. But to that date, Danny had heard from only a handful of colleges. Others shied away because of Heater's lack of size, even though Stalnaker kept a supply of vitamins on hand.

Before the Widen game, a small college coach who liked Heater's talents took Stalnaker aside and offered a suggestion. Why not, he said, turn Danny loose on the state single-game scoring record of 79 points and thus attract some publicity for the unselfish player.

The young coach had reservations about running up a score, but he was sincere in wanting to help his player. After all, he had been by the Heater home on many a winter day watching Danny at endless practice, sometimes in overshoes.

So Stalnaker ordered his team to feed the ball to Heater in the Widen game that night. He told his players they could tip in the ball if they got the chance, but otherwise pass it to Danny. He had no problem getting the Bruins to agree with him.

The strategy almost backfired from the start: For 1:58 into the game they fed Heater but he didn't shoot once. In fact, heavily favored Burnsville was on the short end of the score. Adjustments were made, and Heater began to score on dazzling shots—jumpers and dunks.

In fact, it took him less than three quarters to get his 80th point and claim the state record. Stalnaker had his reserves in the game, but left Heater in. Heater, who was on his way to a 32-rebound game, continued to pour in the points, and even the Widen cheerleaders were offering encouragement.

The coach finally pulled Heater with 10 minutes left to play. But a couple of the starters mentioned that a Pennsylvanian had recently set a national record with 120 points in a game—so why not let Danny shoot for it.

The coach hesitated at first, but then bought the idea. Heater went back in.

By now, Widen was playing a slowdown game.

But Heater continued to dominate. He stole inbound passes, threw in three left-handed hooks in a row, and in a whirlwind finish, scored 55 points in 10 minutes to finish the game with 135.

Note that unlike Wilt Chamberlain, who scored the pro record 100 points in a 48-minute game in 1962, and Bevo Francis, who set the college record in a 40-minute game in 1954, Heater was scoring at a faster clip of 4.2 points per minute to get his 135 in a 32-minute game.

For the game, Heater shot 70 times from the floor and made 53. At the free-throw line he was 29 of 41. Surprisingly he also had 7 assists as Burnsville rolled up 173 points. Three veteran scorekeepers verified all the totals.

After the word got out, Heater received his scholarship to the University of Richmond. But then his luck ran out. His brief career ended after he was injured in an auto accident.

# Ladies Night at Club 100

Lisa Leslie's coach at Morningside High School in Inglewood, Calif., maintained in her senior year that his star could have averaged 50 points a game rather than the very respectable 27.3 that she was recording in the 1989–90 season.

But 50 points a game is a lot for anybody.

Yet after a game on February 7, 1990, Lisa's next-to-last regular-season high school game, one had to wonder if perhaps the coach was correct. Coach Frank Scott had a policy of letting his best senior try to run up an individual score in her last game. But he made a late switch in 1990 because the team had a potentially heated finale coming up against Centennial High School. Instead of having to worry about Centennial getting too physical against Lisa, he decided to turn her loose against hapless South Torrance, a team with a 3–18 record, in the next-to-last.

Even Scott, however, could not have expected what kind of scoring machine his 6-foot-5 center could be. Going into the game, the national scoring record in girls' scholastic basketball was 105 points by Cheryl Miller, who did it at Riverside (Calif.) Poly in 1982 on her way to becoming one of the finest women players in American history.

Scott was more interested in Lisa, whose most points in a game was 40, trying to break the school record of 68 points, if that was possible. But he did tell Lisa that if she scored 25 points a quarter, she could be in a position to break Miller's national record. And the coach passed the message along to Lisa's teammates, too.

"We got together and I told the team what we were trying to do and that they all had to make the sacrifice," he said.

Lisa took the floor, and with help from her teammates, followed the coach's orders, being the focal point of every shot her team would take. Even if they got into position to score, they were to send the ball back to Lisa.

And scored she did, right from the start. She hit jumpers, went into the paint for easy layups, used her height against the outclassed South Torrance team and was deadly at the free-throw when the opponents desperately tried to stop her by fouling her.

She was cool when South Torrance realized what was going on and began to circle her with five defenders, causing her some punishment which included a cut lip.

By the end of the first quarter alone—and keep in mind that high school games are played in 8-minute quarters, unlike the 12-minute quarters in the pros or 20-minute halves in college basketball—Lisa already had 49 points. Her team led 49–6.

South Torrance not only was inferior to Morningside's defending state champions, but was also short-handed because of injuries and bothered by fouls in its quest to stop Lisa.

Lisa was even better in the second quarter, registering 52 points as her team rolled up a 102–24 halftime lead. She now had 101 points, with the only other Morningside point coming on a teammate's free throw.

As Lisa's point total grew, South Torrance's troubles mounted. Two players fouled out, another was injured and only four healthy players were left to contend with Lisa and powerful Morningside.

Lisa had already made 37 of 56 field-goal attempts and hit 27 of 35 shots from the free-throw line. No schoolgirl had ever scored that many free throws in a full game, much less a half.

Cheryl Miller's record could not have been more vulnerable. After all, Lisa was almost 100 points ahead of a record pace and on her way to scoring more points by far than any high school, college or pro player had ever done.

But there was one person who could stop her.

It turned out to be the South Torrance coach, Gilbert Ramirez.

As South Torrance met during its halftime break, the coach figured enough was enough.

He decided to forfeit the game, ending it right there. His team members agreed with him.

Lisa asked the coach to reconsider, giving her at least a chance to break Miller's record. But Ramirez wouldn't relent.

His team did not show for the second half.

The game referees did allow Morningside to begin shooting technical free throws to start the second half as a penalty for South Torrance not taking the floor. Needless to say, Coach Scott sent Lisa to the line. She made four in a row, giving her a game total of 105 points to tie Miller's record.

But the state association ruled that those extra 4 points would not count, because South Torrance officially forfeited at halftime.

Thus Lisa went into the books with a 101-point effort, which was not bad for a half-game's work.

# 13-year-old Scores 272 Points in One Game

In February 1974, a 13-year-old boy in Sweden beat the Americans at their own game. A report came out of Stockholm that Mats Wermelin, age 13, had had a pretty good day.

He scored all 272 of his team's points in a basketball tournament sponsored by a newspaper. The rest of his team concentrated on defense apparently, for the final score was reported as 272–0.

# • II •

# Team Efforts

## U.S. 1960 Olympians:
## Greatest Amateur Team

It was a team of unbelievable potential. How much was probably never fully appreciated until so much of it was fulfilled. And was it ever fulfilled! Four members would make NBA Rookie-Of-the-Year. A man generally considered to be one of the two best guards of all time missed becoming the fifth only because he came up the same year as one of the others. Four others would make NBA All-Star teams.

One would have to look far and wide to find an amateur basketball team better than the 1960 United States Olympic squad. To try would probably be a waste of time.

Consider the talent: The center, Jerry Lucas, was in the midst of a three-time all-America career at Ohio State. The forwards, Terry Dischinger of Purdue and Oscar Robertson of Cincinnati, were also three-time all-Americas. In the backcourt was Jerry West of West Virginia, in the eyes of many still the greatest guard ever to play the game. (In the eyes of many of the rest it is Robertson, who shifted positions upon entering the NBA.) Les Lane, who earned a spot on the team through the old Amateur Athletic Union ranks, started alongside West.

Coming off the bench—a bench that was used early and often—behind Lane was Adrian Smith, who would go on to a long and successful NBA career as Robertson's backcourt mate with the Cincinnati Royals. The team's front-line depth was breathtaking. For 6-foot-11 centers Walt Bellamy and Darrell Imhoff and power forward Bob Boozer, this would be the first time in their lives they played for a club they couldn't start for.

Robertson would be named the NBA's top rookie in 1961, to be followed in successive years by Bellamy, Dischinger and Lucas. West missed out because of Robertson. Boozer also went on to become a solid pro while Imhoff, who had led California to an NCAA title, also logged several strong years.

To coordinate all this talent into a cohesive unit, the choice was Pete Newell, who coached California to the 1959 national championship. Newell, considered one of the great minds of the game, claims Bobby Knight among his disciples. It did not take Newell long to realize his team's ironic weakness—too much talent.

They were so good they were expected to handle the ball all the time. In college, Oscar handled the ball maybe 60 percent of the time. The same for West and Dischinger. Lucas handled it maybe 50 percent of the time. Les Lane was a 24-point scorer in AAU ball. It's not that they were selfish on their other teams; they were good and it was expected of them.

Sid Newell: "You had to get them used to not playing with the ball. That's not easy. You had to create a new habit."

Newell's way of solving the "problem" was to insist during halfcourt practices that no one could shoot until he signaled them to do so by blowing his whistle. That way he slowed them down, even though they could have scored at will, and the individuals melded into a cohesive passing and screening team. This would become evident

*DREAM TEAM: Jerry Lucas (shooting) led the 1960 U.S. Olympic team, one of the finest groups of talent ever assembled in basketball history.*

by the time they reached Rome in September 1960 for the start of the Games.

There were other adjustments to make, such as international rules and playing with the old fashioned European basketball, which resembled a soccer ball because of its panels.

"But these guys were intelligent as well as talented," said Newell. "For example Robertson found that the ball banked in easier than the American ball did and quickly adapted his shot accordingly."

During the pre-Olympic tuneup tour, the squad was too busy bouncing across the country in a fund-raising series. So it wasn't until the Americans arrived in Rome that they really jelled as a team. It took little time, however, to prove this would be a difficult team to beat, even by U.S. Olympic standards. Shooting 60 percent and averaging around 100 points per game, the club breezed toward the finals. Lucas shot an amazing 70-percent-plus for the tournament, including a 14-for-14 game against Japan.

In addition to Russia, solid teams were fielded by Italy and Brazil, evidence that basketball was beginning to catch on more internationally. But, despite their experience, these quintets were no match for the U.S. In fact the same Italian fans who were whistling down the Americans in an earlier game would be cheering the U.S. when it took on Russia in the final.

That showdown presented early problems for the Americans. With a 7-foot-4 center and far more experience in international play, Russia got the U.S. in foul trouble. Newell recalled that every starter had three personals apiece by halftime as he sat them down one after the other. With the abundance of centers and lack of true forwards on his squad, the coach was forced into using some makeshift combinations as the Russians kept the game close.

*NAME GAME: Jerry West was just one of the future pros who filled up the lineup card for the U.S. team at Rome.*

"At halftime," said Newell, "I just told our players, 'We better put this game away so the officials don't take it away.'"

They must have been listening. With the regular starting unit back in to begin the second half, the U.S. outscored Russia with a 25–3 barrage and blew away the second-best amateur team in the world by the final score of 81–57.

The gold medal accomplished, the team dispersed to pursue further professional glory. But the squad did get together one more time. In 1984, the players and coaches were honored at a reunion as the first basketball team selected for the United States Olympic Hall of Fame.

# The Little Green Giants

The nickname was the Green Giants, which may sound a bit presumptuous for a high school of 92 students located in an Illinois farm town of 600 people. But in 1952, Alden-Hebron High more than lived up to its nickname as it captured the attention of the state's basketball fans on its way to capturing the state title in an open tournament that began with 800 teams.

For a town like Hebron, located near the Wisconsin border, to even think that big, it needed a catalyst, and it had one in Russ Ahern, its coach. In 1948, Ahern arrived from a much larger school, Elgin, so he wasn't awed by the enrollment size of opponents. Hebron, with about 60 students, had just consolidated with Alden, about half that size, to form the new school.

Ahern immediately found one advantage of small towns: Four of the starters on his eventual championship team had been together since their early grade-school days in Hebron. They were the 6-foot-1 Judson twins, Paul and Phil, and two 5-foot-11 players, Ken Spooner and Don Willbrandt. Another advantage was that none of the four were farmboys so they had lots of time to spend in the gym, borrowing the keys to practice in the evenings and on Sunday. From Alden came Bill Schulz, a farmboy who grew to become a 6-foot-11 center and blended in well with the foursome by his junior year, 1951–52.

Ahern foresaw what was in store for that season. He began booking major powers and scheduled only one-fourth of the Green Giant games in the petite Hebron facility, which had an undersized playing floor that was set on an old-fashioned theatrical stage at one end of the auditorium. Others began foreseeing things for the school, too. With their controlled fast break and pressing man-to-man defense, the Giants went on a tear at the start of the season and found themselves ranked No. 9 in the state.

They had confidence in themselves, too.

"We knew we were good, especially after we got the No. 9 ranking and saw Danville, a bigger school, was No. 8," recalled Phil Judson, now the coach at Zion-Benton High. "We had beaten Danville by 25 in a tournament."

The Giants' only loss en route to a 24–1 regular season was a 71–68 midseason game to Crystal Lake, which according to Judson was "the only time anyone scored more than 60 against us."

Then he recalled a chalk talk before the first tourney game: "Coach Ahern wrote the number 11 on the blackboard. Then he said, 'You win the next 11 and you'll be state champions.' That's how many games we would have to play to do it."

The Giants swept through the district and regional tourneys, including a victory over Crystal Lake, and earned a trip to the University of Illinois in Champaign for the Sweet 16 finals.

Meanwhile, back in Hebron, townspeople got "March Madness." A third of the population headed for Champaign, and firefighters and police from adjacent towns were needed to protect Hebron.

As usual, Ahern made it clear to his team what was expected in Champaign. "He was very, very determined," recalled Spooner, then a junior like Schulz. "He was very positive that we could win."

Among the Sweet 16 were Champaign High, the local favorite; Rock Island and Quincy—all schools of 1,000 or more students.

Hebron drew Champaign for its opener. It was noisy and nerve-wracking for the smalltown boys in Huff Gymnasium, but they prevailed by 10. They won their next game by 10 and drew Rock Island in the semifinal.

"We were down by 3 at the end of the third quarter," recalled Judson. "Then we came out and scored 15 straight and won by 12."

That put the Giants in the final against Quincy.

"I felt like we had all the fans in the state, except Quincy's, for us," Judson said.

But no fans were involved like Hebron's. At least five ended up in hospitals with illnesses related to excitement, including two girls who had hysteria breakdowns. The final game didn't help quell any nerves. Quincy took Hebron into overtime—the first for the Giants that year.

But Hebron, poised and talented, jumped to a 5-point lead, clamped down on defense and came up a 64–59 winner.

Today, oldtimers in Hebron still talk about the game with reverence and regularity. "Sometimes the younger people think we talk about it too much," said a secretary at Alden-Hebron High who had followed the team to Champaign.

The five starters, who all went to college on basketball scholarships (the Judsons to Illinois, Schulz and Spooner to Northwestern and Willbrandt to Valparaiso), still gather from time to time to remember their team and their coach, who died several years ago. Last summer they were in Hebron for the town's 150th anniversary and helped dedicate a new water tower. Appropriately, the water tower was built to resemble a big basketball.

# Smaller Giants

Undoubtedly the smallest giant in high school basketball history was Beal's Island (Maine) High School, located on an island in the Atlantic Ocean. Beal's Island High had only 11 boys among its student body during the 1950–51 school year. Of them, nine were on the basketball squad. The tenth was the student manager, and the last was the male lead in the rooting section. The star of the team was Stanley Beal.

Beal's High practiced in a tiny gymnasium whose basketball floor measured only 35 × 48 feet, about half the size of a standard professional basketball court. The ceiling was a mere 15 feet above the floor, which made for some straight-arrow shooting.

But in the early 1950's, Beal's made the best of its opportunities. In the 1950–51 season, Beal's ran up victories of 100–59 over Addison, 103–71 over Cherryfield, 105–90 over Jonesboro, 133–56 over Harrington and, in a return match, 141–80 over Cherryfield. Its only defeat going into the state tournament was 38–37 to Vanceboro, a team Beal's had beaten by a 91–46 margin earlier.

In Maine, unlike Illinois, tournament teams are classified according to enrollment, so Beal's Island was bracketed with the state's smallest schools for the annual playoff. Still, Beal's was just about the smallest school to challenge for the state title in its classification.

That year, Beal's Island High School won its sectional honors and gained a berth in the state finals. But an influenza epidemic swept the island and felled most of the team. Clinton High, which had also gained a berth in the finals, was sportsmanlike and allowed the final game to be postponed for six days. Once recovered, the Beal's Island players headed for the mainland and clinched the state title to run their season record to 24–1.

The next season, enrollment at the high school was up to a whopping 23 students and Beal's Island High School continued to bask in glory. In addition to rolling up 159 points in a game against Addison, the team retained its state title.

## The Wonder Team and Its Coach

No wonder they were called the "Wonder Teams." From December 17, 1919, to February 6, 1925, Passaic N.J. High School teams won 159 straight games. That's far better than the longest college and pro streaks combined.

In an era of low-scoring contests, Passaic topped 100 points a dozen times during its streak. Once it crushed a Stamford (Conn) prep school, 145–5. Throughout the streak, it outscored opponents by an average of 59.5 to 20.2.

Passaic's credo was "a strong offense is the best defense." That's a turnabout of the old sports adage, but few could criticize the Passaic coach, Professor Ernest Blood. The late Bill Mokray, a team manager during the streak, who later went on to compile "Mokray's Averages," a statistical aid book used by the NBA, once estimated the Passaic "Wonder Teams" controlled the ball about 70 percent of the time. Needless to say, that put opponents' offenses at a huge disadvantage. Less than half of Passaic's foes during the streak topped 20 points a game.

Meanwhile, Passaic had several players averaging over 20 in an era when a 10-point scorer was considered pretty good. The best undoubtedly were Johnny Roosma and Bobby Thompson. Roosma averaged 28.4 one year and Thompson averaged 30.3 the season after Roosma left. Thompson once scored 64, 31 and 69 points in successive games.

When Roosma and Thompson were teamed up for the 1921–22 season, Passaic was at its best, winning all 33 of its games while outscoring the opposition by an average of 51 points a game.

But the true star of the "Wonder Teams" was its coach. Blood began playing basketball in 1892, when the sport was just one year old and he 20. He started coaching three years later in his native New England and later in Potsdam, New York, where his high school team didn't lose a game to another high school from 1906 to 1915.

Blood moved to Passaic, just west of New York City, in 1918 and immediately toured many classrooms in that milltown's 12-school network. Passaic had only two gyms at the time, but Blood improvised in his search for athletic talent by conducting calisthenics right on the spot during the classroom visits. That way he learned about every potential athlete available to him.

The coach lost little time utilizing the talent. In his first season, 1918–19, Passaic won all 41 games before losing the state championship game. In Passaic's next game, beginning the 1919–20 season, the streak began.

Blood was a remarkable coach, who, as the streak hit high gear, thought nothing of donning a uniform and working out with the boys, despite his 50 years of age. He was a perfectionist. One time, Roosma made 89 straight free throws in practice. Blood, matching him shot for shot, passed him and ran his string to 105.

The winning streak began with a 44–11 thrashing of Newark Junior College. The victories began to roll methodically as Passaic ripped off 25 straight and made it to the state final again. This time Blood pulled a surprise and started a 15-year-old freshman, Fritz Knothe, in the final game. Knothe proved more than adequate and would go on to become one of the top stars during the dynasty's future years.

The next season, Passaic rolled through 31 more victories and the following season added 33 more. Its fame around the Northeast, at least, was spreading. The "Wonder Teams" began searching the Northeast to find the best competition. Once, 9,000 fans saw them play a game in New York City. Before the fourth straight unbeaten season (1922–23) ended, a Passaic game was broadcast over radio. It may have been the first basketball game ever broadcast at any level. And in Passaic, where few could afford a crystal radio set, much less to go on the road and cheer for their heroes, a factory whistle would denote the team's success—two loud blasts for a victory, one long blast in case of defeat.

However, even the threat of one blast was remote. The real tests were few and far between. Once, Montclair High had Passaic down 12–8 at halftime. Knothe, whose right (shooting) arm was so heavily bandaged he could not shoot with it, then came off the bench and pumped in a crucial bucket left-handed and Passaic was off and running to a 31–20 victory. Blood, always ahead of his time, had taught his players to shoot both ways.

After the 1923–24 season, Blood left Passaic for another coaching job. The streak had reached 147. On New Year's Day, 1925, the "Wonder Teams" won their 150th straight. In all, there would be 12 victories after Blood's departure, including one game that was filmed and shown to fans five days later.

Finally, Passaic ran out of wonders. On February 6, 1925, nearby Hackensack High brought the streak to a close with a 39–35 upset.

By then, of course, Roosma and other dynasty members were gone, as was Blood. But it would not be the last time they would be heard from. Roosma, after a career at West Point, was voted into the Basketball Hall of Fame. Flood was also accorded that honor after compiling the astonishing high school coaching record of 1,296–165. In fact the only two coaches elected ahead of him were the legendary Phog Allen of Kansas and Doc Carlson of the University of Pittsburgh.

There's hardly any comparison to Passaic's unbeaten streak in schoolboy cage history. But a few other high schools gave it a try.

Among them are Beaufort, N.C., with 91 victories in a row (through 1962); Kalama, Wash., with 84 (through 1952); Middletown, O., with 76 (through 1958); and Power Memorial, New York City, with 71 (through 1965).

Jerry Lucas was the star for Middletown; Lew Alcindor (now Kareem Abdul-Jabbar) was Power's standout.

# 218 Wins, 0 Defeats

If high-school boys' teams have failed in their attempts to match Passaic's string of victories, a girls' team has had more success. It began to happen in 1947. That year, the girls' varsity basketball team at Baskins (La.) High School displayed obvious improvement in its 1947–48 opening game when it defeated Ogden High, 50–15. In the last game of the previous season, Baskins had lost to Ogden, 35–16.

But the real significance of the victory would not be known for some time to come. As it turned out, the triumph touched off a 218-game winning streak. It wouldn't be until 1953 that Baskins would lose again.

Baskins was a small cattle and cotton town and the local high school had only about 70 girls at the time. But the coach, Willie Edna (Tiny) Tarbutton, worked her players like a maestro in brief one-hour, four-day-a-week practices, teaching the girls a brand of basketball that emphasized intelligence. During the victory string, Baskins High had more fouls than the opposing team only twice.

Baskins compiled a 38–0 record that first season of the streak, followed by 43–0, 45–0, 38–0 and 40–0 records. Baskins was into another winning season in 1952–53 when Winnsboro upset the girls, 33–27. That defeat would be Baskins' only one in 39 games that year.

Along the way there were few challenges and lots of state championships. The 190th triumph—50–48 over Oak Grove High—was one of the few in which Baskins had to come from behind. In that game, Baskins trailed until the final 3½ minutes.

The average game was about 54–23, in Baskins favor. Such runaway scores kept Baskins' individual heroes from compiling any astonishing averages. Usually Tiny

Tarbutton rotated her 18 squad members. But one definite star was 5-foot-10 Mildred Ragsdale, who averaged 21.7 points though she played only about half of each game during five years with the team. Mildred had made the varsity when she was in the eighth grade. She was all-state three years. Her performance is put in perspective when it is pointed out that she scored only 159 points less than all of the opposing *teams* she played against.

Another star was Dixie Baskins, who also played five years. She never played in a losing game. Baskins High was 204–0 during her varsity career.

But the real hero was the coach. Her record was an astounding 343–12 for her first nine seasons. In eight of those campaigns, Baskins High won the state championship.

# 212 Points Well Taken

Essex Community College had already totaled 100 points and was playing the game it had primed itself for all season.

Earlier in the 1973–74 season, the Essex Community Wolverines had scored 160 points, and at other times 141, 139, 132 and 130 points. They were averaging 108 while compiling a 17–3 record.

Their opponent, Englewood Cliffs, meanwhile, was just trying to survive, which it wasn't doing a very good job of, because the school would be out of business before 1974 came to an end.

Essex Community befuddled the Cliffs right from the start, throwing a zone press defense against a team expecting man-to-man. When Cliffs adjusted for the press, Essex switched to man-to-man. Also, Essex's continuity-pattern offense picked up points when the defense did not.

Essex scored the first 26 points of the game. Stanley Williams scored the first 6 points on steals alone. Essex took a 110–29 halftime lead and was rotating players constantly. For comic relief, near the end of the first half, the Cliffs' coach protested too vociferously over goal-tending calls and got penalized 5 free throws (which Essex made) and got ordered off the floor, the 81-point defeat notwithstanding.

At the half, some players made a special request to their coach, Cleo Hill. They asked if they could shoot for the national junior college record, which was believed to be 202 points.

"I told them I didn't think they could do it," recalled Hill, who had seen more than his share of record-makers in his time. The coach had played as a pro with the National Basketball Association St. Louis Hawks, who had such high-scoring stars as Bob Pettit and played in an era of record-breaking opponents, such as Wilt Chamberlain. As a collegian, Hill was a predecessor to Earl Monroe, one of college basketball's most prolific scorers ever at the time, at high-scoring Winston-Salem College in North Carolina.

As it turned out in the second half this January night, however, Essex started slowly. Perhaps the Wolverines' goal of another 100-points-plus half seemed unreasonable.

But Englewood Cliffs College was by now mentally beaten as well as very undermanned. It also helped that the Wolverines' bench, which was being used liberally, was better than the Cliffs' starting lineup and just by being so fresh added to the pressure.

The Essex fast break began to click again, the defensive net tightened once more and the points began to fall again. In gobs.

The fact that Essex's court in Newark, New Jersey, was small made the trips to the basket more frequent, too.

With 15 minutes left in the 40-minute game, Essex Community huddled during a time out and got the word from a radio announcer that the team indeed was within reach of the records.

The Wolverines decided to go for it.

Scoring furiously, Essex Community still needed 21 points in the last three minutes. It got much more than that, and wound up with 29.

Final score of the game:

Essex County Community College, 210
Englewood Cliffs College, 67

Hill just shook his head in disbelief as the overworked scoreboard tried to keep up with his nonstop team. As he would recall later, remembering that he looked up often. "It was like an adding machine."

For the game, Essex Community shot an astonishing 97 for 129 on their field-goal attempts. One of the Essex players, Lou Grimsley, made 22 of 26 attempts.

The Wolverines were also 16 for 22 from the free-throw line. They dominated the backboards with 89 rebounds.

Grimsley was the high scorer with 44 points. But four teammates also scored in the 20's, and three others were in the high teens.

For the 1973–74 season, Essex Community finished with 21 games over 100 points—and, of course, one over 200.

## The Sophomores Win It All

Nat Holman learned his basketball lessons well as a star for the Original Celtics teams of the 1920s. And later he applied those lessons to teams of his own which he coached at City College of New York, where he was one of the first coaches to utilize the sidewalk talent so abundant in the big metropolitan communities. At CCNY, Holman coached for over four decades and his list of standouts is long indeed.

But promise was all Holman had to work with when he assembled his 1949–50 team. He had a couple of seniors named Irwin Dambrot and Norm Mager to work with, and he had to rotate four sophomores—Ed Warner, Ed Roman, Floyd Layne and Al Roth—in and out of the lineup. It was a promising team—the sophomores were good ones—but it was a group that would take some time. The critics attached a look-see tag to the CCNY quintet. During the season, the Beavers would not make the rankings.

They weren't a bad team, losing only five games. But they weren't standouts, either.

Holy Cross had Bob Cousy, Southern Cal had Bill Sharman, Kansas had Clyde Lovellette, Villanova had Paul Arizin and Temple had Bill Mlkvy—superstars all. The sportswriters didn't need any Irwin Dambrots and untried sophomores to get excited about.

Somehow, though, the Beavers were selected to play in the post-season National Invitation Tournament at Madison Square Garden. The CCNY quintet at least was good enough and interesting enough to draw some of its own fans to help fill the early-round nights at the Garden, despite their lack of national stature.

The Beavers were pitted against defending champs, San Francisco University, in the opener of the 1950 NIT. Somehow, CCNY pulled off a 65–46 upset. It made the critics sit up and take notice; but then again out-of-town teams, especially the long-distance travelers, get stunned in early-round games.

CCNY's youthful club earned the critics' support, however, after it crushed powerful University of Kentucky, with its 7-foot center Bill Spivey, in the second round. The 89–50 rout was one of the worst in Kentucky's heralded basketball history. It was a good Kentucky team, too. The Wildcats had won the NCAA in 1949 and would win it again in 1951.

CCNY conquered Duquesne, 62–52, and Bradley, 69–61, to earn the NIT title in real upset fashion.

Immediately after the NIT finale, Garden officials began making plans to host the NCAA tournament, too. The NCAA selection committee was duly impressed by the Beavers' performance in the NIT and decided to make them a last-minute entry.

The next week, the Beavers continued their march through March into college basketball history.

The sophomores began playing like the superstars they would become and the 6-foot-4 Dambrot was outstanding at forward. The Beavers chipped their way through a tough Ohio State team, to win the NCAA opener 56–55. Then they upset North Carolina State, 78–73. Before they knew it, they had another date with Bradley, just two weeks after surprising the Peoria, Ill., team in the NIT finale.

The Bradley Braves had a couple of All-America candidates in Paul Unruh and Gene Melchiorre. The Braves were a stable club that seemed to have learned its lessons in its first defeat by CCNY. The Beaver sophomores were well scouted before the March 28 encounter.

But again the two teams played a tight game. Down to the final seconds, the Cinderella team from the streets of New York held only a one-point margin. But the players held their poise, too. Moments later, CCNY scored two more points and clinched a 71–68 victory, the NCAA title and a historic double. In coming years, NIT and NCAA schedules conflicted so the double could not be duplicated.

Also in the years to come, New York City basketball at the college level would go downhill. Some of the same CCNY players were involved in messy gambling scandals. No other New York City team has won the NCAA since then. But on March 28, 1950, no other New York City team could have been happier.

# • III •

# Sharp Shooters

## Peaking for the Playoffs: Michael Jordan

Though it was early in what would become a fabled professional career, Michael Jordan could not consider his 1985–86 season with the Chicago Bulls much of a success. In the 1984–85 season, after he had dropped out of the University of North Carolina to sign a huge pro contract, he had caught the NBA by storm. As a rookie, he averaged 28.2 points and another 29.3 in the playoffs and the league knew it had another young superstar on the horizon. Jordan was the league's rookie of the year and made second-team all-NBA.

He looked every bit the player who would later sign a $26 million contract and make more than that on endorsements, because he was as charismatic off the court as he was on it as a high-scoring guard with unbelievable moves on offense and defense.

But in 1985–86, Jordan suffered a broken foot, disabling for any pro but especially for a high-jumping one, and played in only 18 games during the regular season. He averaged 22.7 points, good for most pros, but not one who would make 30- and 40-point games his norm.

The injury came early in the season, however, and the 6-foot-6 guard was back at the end of the season in time to help the Bulls clinch fourth place in their division and barely make the playoffs.

Not that there was much hope in the playoffs. The Bulls' opponent was the Boston Celtics, the team with the best record in the league that season, and the first two games of the best-of-5 series were scheduled for Boston Garden.

What else was there for Jordan to do but give his best?

He certainly did that.

In the first game, Jordan scored 49 points, almost half of his team's total as the Bulls lost, convincingly, 123–104.

Three days later, on a Sunday afternoon in front of a national TV audience, Jordan and the Bulls would give it another go in Boston. For Jordan, that April 20th day was go-go-go.

But beating Boston in Boston is a tough playoff assignment. That's when Larry Bird and Kevin McHale of the Celtics take over. This day was no different as the Celtic stars would match the Bulls shot for shot, with Bird (36) and McHale (27) combining for 63 points—a championship effort.

What wasn't expected was what Jordan would do to offset that tandem, even though the fans got a hint of it in the first half when Jordan scored 30 points.

In the third quarter, Jordan had more than an inkling that he was on fire as he pulled his team within 65–55 with a nifty soft 20-footer from the corner. "All day, baby," he said. "Allll day."

His day was not over.

Jordan matched the Celtics shot for shot throughout the third and fourth periods, and tied the game with no time left with two free throws to send the game into overtime.

If Jordan had one bad moment during the game, it came with 6 seconds left in the first overtime when he

*ABOVE THE REST: Michael Jordan's scoring feats have awed NBA followers like no one since Wilt Chamberlain.*

missed a 15-footer that would have given his team a 127–125 lead and most likely a sure victory.

But he was not done in a game that dragged on into a second overtime, spread over 3 hours 5 minutes. Jordan kept pumping away, both from the floor and the foul line.

But in the end, Boston prevailed as the Celtics usually do at playoff time. The Celtics survived through the waning moments to win, 135–131.

That score stat will be lost in history, however. What will be remembered is Jordan's scoreline: 63 points, to break a 34-year-old playoff record set by Elgin Baylor, who had 61 for the Los Angeles Lakers against the Celtics in 1962. In 53 minutes on the court, Jordan made 22 of 41 shots and 19 of 21 from the free-throw line. He also found time to dole out six assists to teammates.

Even Bird, for whom playoff heroics are commonplace, could not resist saying later: "It was probably one of the greatest efforts in the Boston Garden, on national TV and in the playoffs."

# Longest Shot in Pro History

Coaches are the first people to tell their players not to quit until the final buzzer goes off. But anyone could sympathize with Indiana Pacer coach Larry Staverman for departing early from a wearing game with the old Dallas Chaparrals on November 13, 1967.

Staverman had just watched John Beasley shoot a jump shot to put the Chaparrals ahead with one second to play in a hard-fought game. It gave Dallas a 118–116 lead. So Staverman headed for his team's locker room to get ready for the trip back to Indianapolis. Across the court, Beasley's teammates were hugging him and proclaiming victory.

But in the single second that remained, a hardened little clutch player named Jerry Harkness was about to make history. Harkness, a guard, had once helped lead underdog Loyola of Chicago to an NCAA title. He had had a tryout with the New York Knicks in 1963 but didn't make it into more than five games. They said he didn't have an outside shot, which was probably true. The 6-foot-2 Harkness was an infighter, a player who burrowed underneath for his baskets and earned his assignments for his ability to pass and play defense.

After being cut by the Knicks, Harkness took a job with Quaker Oats as a physical fitness instructor. But the emergence of the American Basketball Association rekindled his interest in the pro game. He decided to make one more try. The Indiana Pacers gave him a chance. Despite an abundance of good shooters at the guard position, Harkness made the team.

In Dallas that November night, Harkness was hanging under the Chaparral basket after Beasley made his heartbreaking shot. Harkness moved off to one side as teammate Oliver Darden inbounded a pass to him.

Under the rules, the clock does not start until the player on the playing floor (in bounds) touches the ball. There was only one thing to do in this case and that was to heave the ball downcourt upon getting it—in hopes, perhaps, of having the receiver get fouled.

Which is what Harkness did. He pretty much hooked the ball as soon as it came to him. To try and catch it first, or to dribble, would run out the clock, obviously.

While Staverman headed for the exit and the Chaparrals were patting Beasley on the back, the ball lofted downcourt toward the basket. Once the ball is in the air, a basket can count even if the final buzzer goes off.

Harkness' throw went in.

Under the ABA rules, the shot was made from beyond the 25-foot line and thus counted as a three-pointer, not the conventional two-point field goal. Not only did Harkness score, but he won the game for Indiana—119–118.

Since Harkness was just inside the end line of the 94-foot court, a quick measurement was called for. His long shot was credited at 92 feet—farther than any professional shot had ever gone.

Discouraged but not humorless, the Chaparrals decided to paint an ABA insignia on the floor at the spot from which Harkness had launched his historic missile. Then someone in the Dallas organization added new emphasis to the spot—he circled it in black.

Soon Harkness would not be a threat to ABA teams any more. He just didn't have a good enough outside shot to make it in pro ball.

The National Basketball Association has had its share of dramatic long shots, too.

And strange as it may seem, the longest and most famous ones have been made by some of the best-known players.

Bob Cousy, the great ex-Boston Celtic guard, is believed to be the distance record holder with a 79-footer back in 1953. But his equally gifted ex-teammate, Bill Sharman, lofted a 70-footer in the 1957 All-Star game.

For pure drama, though, Jerry West's 60-footer in the 1970 playoff series between the Los Angeles Lakers and New York Knicks rates with the best.

At the end of the third game, Laker star West lifted his knee after a short dribble behind the midcourt line and let fly with a fantastic 60-footer. It tied a very tight ballgame with no time left on the clock. Dave De-Busschere of the Knicks merely sank to the floor. Meanwhile, Wilt Chamberlain had rushed off the court thinking the game was over. And the Laker sportscaster announced it as 80 feet; like everyone else, he was swept away by the excitement.

# College Long Shots

There's a small gold cross imbedded into the basketball floor of an obsolete gymnasium in Tuscaloosa, Ala., and it's safe to say that more shots have been taken from that exact spot than any place (except at foul lines) in the basketball world. The "X" marks the precise spot from which George Linn, then a junior at the University of Alabama, sent flying the most famous long shot in college basketball history.

There were about 20 seconds remaining on the first-half clock when the University of North Carolina team took a rebound off the Alabama board and returned the ball downcourt to scoring range during a January 4, 1955, ballgame. The site of the game was Foster Auditorium on the Alabama campus.

About 12 seconds later Carolina's All-America Lennie Rosenbluth missed and so did a tip-in that followed. Alabama's 6-foot-4 Linn muscled in for the rebound and got a firm hold on the ball. The shooting and rebounding had eaten up most of those final eight seconds. Linn was to the right of the backboard, just about on one of the free-throw lines, when he came down with the ball. As he turned toward his own basket, he quickly caught sight of the red portion on the scoreboard clock, indicating there was time left in the half.

The partisan crowd screamed for Linn to shoot.

Linn shot all right—the length of the court.

And the ball went in.

Visiting coach Frank McGuire went out and put his foot down on the exact spot where Linn released his shot. That gave Alabama officials a chance to measure the distance accurately.

With the preciseness of a surveyor, Alabama coach

Johnny Dee and others figured the distance. Dee's calculations are good to know for future long shots.

"For those not too familiar with basketball courts, here are some figures," he explained later. "The maximum length for a court is 94 feet. Alabama's was the maximum. The backboards are four feet from the end lines, leaving only 86 feet from the face of one backboard to the other."

Linn was given credit for an 84-foot-11-inch toss, leaving only 13 inches for improvement. Of course, Dee was not making allowances for angles. But few other coaches have staked out claims for long shots with such preciseness. Until some coach does, Linn's feat holds.

The "longest and greatest basket in the history of basketball," Dee described it. However, when the final score was posted that January 4th, Alabama had, despite Linn's long toss, lost, 77–55.

In the years that have passed, the gym has been turned over to the intramural department. Just about every incoming freshman has placed his foot firmly on the gold cross and let fly with a basketball, hoping to duplicate Linn's shot.

# The 5-Foot-4 Free-Throw Giant

The thought of a great shoot-out in basketball brings forth visions of lithe giants, twisting under the hoop or hovering over each other as they unleash shots at 25 feet out. Harold (Bunny) Levitt just doesn't fit the bill. He is only as rangy as a 5-foot-4-inch man can be.

Still, Abe Saperstein, the founder of the Harlem Globetrotters took Levitt on exhibition tour with him for several years in the 1930s, at their peak. Bunny's job was to take on all comers in well-publicized halftime foul-shooting contests. The challenger who could beat Bunny in 100 attempts at the charity line would win $1,000. Anyone who knew how tight-fisted Saperstein could be would appreciate how flawless Bunny was. Saperstein was not a man to let $1,000 slip through his hands.

In his time, Bunny had about 400 halftime challengers. The best anyone ever did was to make 86 free throws, and that was a seasoned shooter who kept following the Trotters across the country in pursuit of the prize money. Levitt remembers the determined opponent hitch-hiking after them. But the challenger's efforts were in vain. The *worst* Levitt ever did was 96. He averaged 98, and sometimes he hit all 100. The $1,000 remained untouched.

Bunny Levitt had a reputation to protect. He announced himself as the "World's Free-Throw Champion," and everyone from Ripley of "Believe It Or Not" to Saperstein of the Trotters was willing to agree, as long as Bunny came through. And even when compared to more recent marks, Levitt's records hold up. Most of the great foul shooters in professional basketball make 80 to 85 percent of their attempts. The best—ex-Boston Celtic star Bill Sharman and pro ace Rick Barry—have reached the 88-percent plateau with some consistency

*TOUCH OF CLASS: Bunny Levitt was the king of free-throw shooters, despite his height.*

over their careers. For Levitt in his prime, 100-for-100 in a workout or exhibition was not unusual. "I never quit in practice till I have thrown 100 baskets without a miss," he told a reporter.

Levitt obviously had an edge on the professional players because he could spend most of his time practicing from the line. And he had begun turning foul shooting into an art while still a youngster.

Bunny figured it should take him no more than 15 minutes to shoot 100 free throws. He could dump them in so fast, he sometimes needed more than one assistant to feed the ball back to him. He had been known to make a thousand baskets in two and a half hours, with the right help. He compared that feat to lifting a ton of weight and moving it 15 feet.

But there was one occasion in April of 1935 when Levitt needed more time. That was when he was engaged in one of the most important contests in his life. The National Amateur Athletic Association scheduled a huge match in Chicago, which happened to be Levitt's hometown then. The site was the Von Steuben gym. About 30 baskets were set up for the long list of contestants. The rules were simple: you had to shoot within a prescribed time limit, and you shot until you missed twice. The rules were in Bunny's favor because of his rapid shooting drills and his consistency.

With his fingertips sanded for smoothness and his concentration fully fixed on the forward rim of the basket, Levitt began methodically firing away at 7 P.M. in his usual underhand style.

As assistants kept feeding him the ball, he wiggled into his stance, twirled each pass-in till he found the exact center of the ball and the same seam, and then put up the ball. He made 100 baskets with hardly any effort. But he was careful to follow his own rule, "After the first

100 throws, try not to try too hard; or else the concentration will cramp your muscles and mind, and tire you out."

Bunny fired away . . . 200 . . . 300 . . . 400. As he approached 500 consecutive throws without a miss, his ballboys were falling to the wayside, worn out from the monotonous "swish . . . swish . . . swish." Extra retrievers were enlisted; before the night was over he would go through 15 of them.

Levitt was still in the groove after 499 straight successes. But at that point, without an explanation, he missed—his first of the night. "I don't know what happened," he would say later. "It just rolled around the rim. I didn't even know what the count was at the time."

Under the rules, Levitt would get one more miss before his official count was entered in the AAU log. He continued to swish baskets without a miss until nearly all of the 2,000 spectators had left the gym. It was well past midnight and he was compiling another remarkable string. At about 2:30 in the morning, though, the officials were getting tired and the janitor was getting impatient. Finally the janitor called a halt. Bunny was just coming off his 371st in a row, giving him 870 of 871.

Bunny pleaded with the janitor for more time, but the cleanup man won out. He ordered the gym shut down.

As Levitt gathered his belongings and the historic ball, he noticed that his stubby fingers, after seven and a half hours of shooting, had worn an eighth of an inch depressions into the leather covering at the points where he gripped it. That ball is now in the Basketball Hall of Fame in Springfield, Mass.

No one has ever come close to breaking Levitt's record of 499. And it may never be bettered, according to Bunny. "Nobody else is that crazy," he says.

But there have been two notable performances since

1935. One came in 1936, when Bunny made 561 straight in practice. The other string, made in Chicago in 1948, was accomplished in front of an audience. Bunny Levitt made exactly 499 in a row again!

## The Long Bomb That Fizzled

When Adam Coffman of Greensburg (Pa.) High School hit the target 91 feet away against powerful Farrell High during the 1953–54 season, a collective gasp went through the crowd.

No, not because history was in the making in the important game against the state champions. But because Coffman was standing out of bounds when he tossed the ball downcourt.

He had meant it to be a long pass, not a shot.

# Hitting a Double in
# Individual Scoring and Team Winning

It's not easy to be an outstanding team player and a great individual scorer at the same time in basketball. One only has to compare two columns in the National Basketball Association's record book—team champions and scoring champions—to learn that.

For a ballplayer to be listed in both columns in the same year is exceptional. Only three different players have accomplished the double since the NBA began play in 1946–47.

The first to hit the "double" was Joe Fulks, a super-shooter for the Philadelphia Warriors, in that initial NBA season. He averaged 23.2 points to top the league as the Warriors won the title. The next person to fit into both categories was George Mikan, the bespectacled Minneapolis Laker center. Mikan averaged 28.3 in 1948–49 and 27.4 in 1949–50 while leading his team to back-to-back NBA titles.

Only one man has hit the "double" since Mikan's dominance of the then 10-team league.

The lone exception was Kareem Abdul-Jabbar, then known as Lew Alcindor, and his accomplishment should stand out even more than those of the oldtimers. Jabbar came into the NBA in 1969–70 when the Bucks were only a year old. Averaging 28.8 points a game, he finished second in the 17-franchise league. Everyone had figured the super 7-footer could score after his vaunted career as a three-time high-school and three-time college all-America. But to expect a 22-year-old rookie to lead a two-year-old team to the brink of an NBA championship was more than the wildest optimists could envision.

As a rookie, Jabbar carried the Bucks right into the

*PLAYING OVER THEIR HEADS: Kareem Abdul-Jabbar, known as Lew Alcindor before he got to the pros, had established his name at UCLA long before he became pro basketball's all-time scorer.*

Eastern Division finals with the New York Knicks. The Bucks ran out of miracles in that series and bowed to the team that went on to the NBA championship. Some fans booed the fledgling superstar—chanting "Goodbye, Lewie, Goodbye, Lewie, We're sorry to see you go"—as he was humbled by a great Knick performance in front of the crowd at Madison Square Garden, where once his home town crowds had cheered him at high-school games. But the more intelligent fans that day knew he would be back.

Milwaukee, switched to the Western Division for the 1970–71 season, ran away from its regular-season opposition as it won over 80 percent of its games. Jabbar won the scoring title with a 31.7 average—almost a full three points better than veteran John Havlicek of the Boston Celtics. Big Lewis made 57.7 percent of his shots from the floor. He was an easy choice for Most Valuable Player honors, making it the biggest landslide vote since the award was begun in 1956.

Scoring titles, winning percentages and MVP honors are of little value, however, if a team doesn't reach the final goal of winning the NBA title. Jabbar was prepared. He sacrificed his scoring in three gruelling series—against San Francisco, Los Angeles and finally Baltimore—but grabbed a fraction under 20 rebounds a game. When it was all over, the Bucks had their title and Jabbar had his distinction of being the only NBA player in more than two decades to lead the league in scoring the year his team won the title.

To accomplish the feat in college basketball is an even more difficult assignment. There are about 300 major college basketball teams and 64 of them compete for the prestigious NCAA championship each March. To outscore the other stars of that many teams and still wind up with the NCAA team trophy almost defies the odds.

*BORN TO WIN: Kareem Abdul-Jabbar was the star of the Lakers' long winning streak.*

Players like Jabbar, whose UCLA team won three NCAA titles, didn't come close to winning the scoring titles. Neither did players like Jerry Lucas or Bill Russell.

But one player did.

The lone exception was Clyde Lovellette, a mammoth 6-foot-9 Kansas star. A native of Terre Haute, Ind., Lovellette was a strongman type of center in all three of his varsity seasons for the Jayhawks. As a sophomore, he averaged almost 22 points for a so-so team. Both Lovellette's average and the team record improved in his junior year. Then, as a senior he blossomed.

That season—1951–52—Lovellette led the nation in scoring with a near-record 28.4 average. Meanwhile, playing tough competition, the Jayhawks lost only two games and were invited to the NCAA tournament.

The tourney is made up of the nation's elite, obviously, so points don't come easy. Still, Lovellette took charge and averaged 35.3 points for his four games. It wasn't until the 1965 NCAA playoffs that his average was topped. With Lovellette unstoppable, Kansas breezed into the finale and whipped St. John's, 80–63.

Lovellette had his double—the scoring title and the NCAA title. To date, no one has come close to duplicating the feat.

*THE BIG TWO: In the 1960s, pro basketball revolved around two players—Bill Russell (left) and Wilt Chamberlain (right) going for the ball.*

# • IV •

# Winners

## Big-Game Hunters: Russell and "Magic"

At the end of the 1956 college basketball season, a slim, 6-foot-9 center named Bill Russell led his University of San Francisco team to its second straight NCAA championship. That December, he led the United States squad to an Olympic title in Melbourne, Australia. Then he joined the Boston Celtics, whose season was already in progress, and got in 48 regular-season games before leading the Celtics to their first pro title in 1957—hardly a year after playing for the NCAA title.

Only a handful of players have ever been part of the NCAA-Olympic-NBA title swoop, and only Russell did it in such short a period of time.

But such was the stuff that Russell, the ultimate defensive center in pro basketball history, was made of. Once Russell, who years before had been cut from his high school basketball team, made the top, he stayed there. In 13 seasons in the NBA, he was the key player on Celtic teams that won the NBA title 11 times and reached the championship series one other time.

Teams that Russell played for in college won their last 56 games. His Olympic team was undefeated. He joined a Celtic team that had a 39–33 record the season before and was a loser in the quarterfinal of post-season play,

*THE MAGIC TOUCH: Earvin (Magic) Johnson was the catalyst for the Lakers, the winningest pro basketball team of the 1980s.*

after finishing fourth in their division during the regular season.

With Russell in the lineup, the Celtics won nine straight division titles in addition to all their NBA titles.

In all, Celtic teams that Russell played for won 70.5 percent of their regular-season games and 63.9 percent of their playoff games.

No wonder that when Russell retired after the 1968–69 season, it was said that no one would match his startling success on the basketball court.

Earvin Johnson was a 9-year-old growing up in Lansing, Michigan, at the time Russell retired. He, too, would grow to be 6-foot-9.

And just as Russell was unusual at center as a small 6-foot-9, Johnson would become unusual at guard at 6-foot-9. Just as Russell would turn games around with rebounding, blocked shots and intimidating defense, Johnson learned to spur offenses with another underrated skill—the assist.

While Johnson, who along the way was renamed "Magic," didn't match Russell's NCAA-Olympic-NBA titles triple, he had a unique one of his own.

In 1977, he led Lansing Everett High School to the state championship in Michigan. As a college sophomore two years later, he led Michigan State to the NCAA title. Then he dropped out of Michigan State to turn pro, was the first draft choice of the Los Angeles Lakers, and at age 20, led the Lakers to the NBA title.

And "led them" is the right phrase.

Before Johnson joined the Lakers, they had posted a respectable 47–35 record and lost in the quarterfinals of the NBA playoffs, four games to one. Johnson, like Russell, started out his pro career with a talented team that just needed a spark. Johnson provided it. In his rookie year, the Lakers were 60–22, the best record in the NBA. His fine playmaking, in addition to his catlike steals on defense and 18-point scoring average, helped carry the Lakers to the top.

But it was in the playoffs that Johnson showed his magic. On May 14, 1980, with his team struggling against the Philadelphia 76ers at the Forum in Inglewood, California, Johnson hit a low point and made 10 turnovers, an NBA playoffs finals record. The Lakers managed to win and take a 3–2 lead in the best-of-7 series. But things did not look good for the Lakers, who had to go to Philadelphia next. Kareem Abdul-Jabbar, the Lakers' star center, was injured and unlikely to start.

The Lakers, however, gambled and put Johnson, their star guard, at center. Magic responded: He scored 42 points, had 15 rebounds and even collected 7 assists as the Lakers overpowered the 76ers, 123–107, to win the game and the title. It was Johnson's first game at center.

In just four years time, Johnson had been named the most valuable player of state high school, NCAA and NBA championship series.

As for Russell's success being impossible to match, consider this:

Through the 1989–90 season, Johnson's 11th in the NBA, the Lakers won 10 division titles, including nine in a row, just like Russell. Johnson's teams won five NBA titles and reached the final series three other times. Until Johnson came along, no NBA team had won back-to-back titles two years in a row since 1969, Russell's last season. The Lakers did it in 1988.

And as for being a winner, with Johnson on the court for 11 seasons, the Lakers won 74.2 percent of their regular-season games and 68.5 percent of their playoff games, a couple of statistics that even Bill Russell would have to look up to.

# Sharman's Coaching Hat Trick: Titles in ABL, ABA and NBA

There was never any question that Bill Sharman was a winner.

As Bob Cousy's running mate at guard for the great Boston Celtic dynasty of the 1950s, Sharman collected enough championship rings to stock a small jewelry store.

But while he played, Sharman was learning the game from the masters—coach Red Auerbach, playmaker Cousy, defensive standout Bill Russell, and the other basketball brains who made the Celtics the team they were.

When Sharman's playing days ended, he set out on a coaching career of his own. It would bring him a piece of history—and more championship rings—that may never be matched.

In his first year as a professional coach (1961–62), Sharman led the Cleveland Pipers to a title in the fledgling American Basketball League. ABL Coach of the Year? Bill Sharman. The ABL did not "fledge" enough, however; the league went out of business before any other hop-scotching coaches could drop in and win a title.

Sharman went into college coaching for a while, then got back to the big leagues with the San Francisco Warriors. After a couple of seasons, Sharman took over the Los Angeles franchise in the ABA. In 1970, that franchise became the Utah Stars.

In three years' time, Sharman had turned the team into a sure winner. The Stars went through the 1970–71 season with an impressive 57–27 record, then won some hard-fought playoff series to win the ABA title. ABA Coach of the Year? Bill Sharman.

The Los Angeles Lakers, quick to see his genius,

## LOS ANGELES LAKERS' RECORD

### 33-Game Win Streak
### (Nov. 5, 1971—Jan. 7, 1972)

| LAKERS | | OPP. |
|---|---|---|
| 110 | Baltimore | 106 |
| 105 | At Warriors | 89 |
| 103 | New York | 96 |
| 122 | At Chicago | 109 |
| 143 | At Philadelphia | 103 |
| 115 | Seattle | 107 |
| 130 | At Portland | 108 |
| 128 | Boston | 115 |
| 108 | Cleveland | 90 |
| 106 | Houston | 99 |
| 112 | Milwaukee | 105 |
| 139 | At Seattle | 115 |
| 132 | Detroit | 113 |
| 138 | Seattle | 121 |
| 124 | At Boston | 111 |
| 131 | At Philadelphia | 116 |
| 123 | Portland | 107 |
| 125 | At Houston | 120 |
| 124 | At Warriors | 111 |
| 126 | Phoenix | 117(OT) |
| 104 | Atlanta | 95 |
| 129 | At Portland | 114 |
| 129 | Warriors | 99 |
| 132 | At Phoenix | 106 |
| 154 | Philadelphia | 132 |
| 117 | At Buffalo | 103 |
| 127 | At Baltimore | 120 |
| 137 | Houston | 115 |
| 105 | Buffalo | 87 |
| 122 | At Seattle | 106 |
| 122 | Boston | 113 |
| 113 | At Cleveland | 103 |
| 134 | At Atlanta | 90 |

beckoned him back to his old hometown for the following season. The Lakers were notorious for their strange mixture of great talent and no titles. They had had their share of good coaches in the past, but no one had made them win in proportion to their talent.

In 1971–72, Sharman did.

That season, the Lakers established eight major NBA

*CALLING THE SHOTS: Bill Sharman hit the triple in basketball coaching at the pro level.*

records, including the most victories (69) and an astounding 33-game victory streak. Also among their accomplishments was a triumph over the San Francisco Warriors by 69 points—widest margin in history. Only once during the regular season did the Lakers fail to score 100 points, giving them another impressive record in an era when defense was being emphasized.

But Sharman's most appreciated feat was to guide the Lakers to the NBA title which they had evaded for so long.

NBA Coach of the Year? Bill Sharman.

# Equaling the Free-Throw
# Without-a-Miss Record

The most free throws made without a miss in a professional basketball game is 23, a total set by Rick Barry when he was with the Oakland Oaks of the American Basketball Association in 1969. The NBA record is just 19 for 19.

But a year after Barry's startling display, a boy named Scott Malaney could hold his head as high as Barry. On December 18, 1970, Malaney also went 23-for-23 from the foul line as he led his Portage (Mich.) Northern High School team to a 70–56 victory over its crosstown rival, Central. The 6-foot-4 senior couldn't have done much better.

Another hot-handed prep star was John Bobalik of Wellsville, Ohio—the same town that produced Bevo Francis. In a game against Carrollton High in 1970, Bobalik connected on all 22 of his free-throw attempts *and* on all eight of his field-goal tries for a perfect 30-for-30 shooting night.

ON THE LINE: *Rick Barry had the finishing touch almost every time he went to the free-throw line.*

# The Super Pressure Shooters

Any college basketball player can pump up his personal statistics with the help of an easy schedule and a generous home-town statistician. But to do it before a national audience in a nationally important tournament game is something else.

Undoubtedly the greatest individual shooting exhibition under tournament conditions was the 21-for-22 field-goal display that UCLA's Bill Walton made against Memphis State University in the crucial championship game of the 1973 NCAA finals. Not only did almost everything Walton put up go in, but his shots were a variety of hooks, jumpers, tip-ins and tough layups in a crowd of talented defenders. A slight favorite going into the game, UCLA came out an 87–66 winner.

That same year in the other major post-season college tournament there was another superb shooting exhibition. In the National Invitation Tournament in Madison Square Garden, John Shumate of Notre Dame made 20 straight field-goal tries.

# A Record 139 Wins in a Row

From the time anyone ever saw Bill Walton on a basketball court, it was obvious the young man was a winner in the truest sense of the word. He was the key, of course, to the 88-game victory streak compiled by UCLA during his sophomore, junior and senior years.

But Walton was even a bigger winner than that: He actually played for teams that won 139 games in a row in high school and college.

As a junior at Helix High School in San Diego, Calif., Walton led his team to a 19-game winning streak spread

*NEAR PERFECT: Bill Walton of UCLA had a shooting night like no player in history in the final game of the NCAA tournament.*

over the latter part of the season. Then as a senior, he was the star of a quintet that went 33–0. The two great back-to-back years won him High School All-America recognition.

During Bill's first season at UCLA, freshmen weren't eligible for the varsity. But teaming with Keith Wilkes and others, Walton played for freshman teams that compiled a 20–0 season.

Walton joined the varsity for the 1971–72 season after UCLA had already touched off the record winning streak of 88.

But as a sophomore, he was the star of teams that won 30 straight of their own. He repeated his success as a junior—another perfect 30–0.

The Bruins had gone through some tough games—

# THE 88-GAME STREAK

## 1970–71

| | | OPP. |
|---|---|---|
| UCLA 74 | Santa Barbara | 61 |
| *UCLA 64 | Southern California | 60 |
| *UCLA 69 | Oregon | 68 |
| *UCLA 67 | Oregon St. | 65 |
| *UCLA 94 | Oregon St. | 64 |
| *UCLA 74 | Oregon | 67 |
| *UCLA 57 | Washington St. | 53 |
| *UCLA 71 | Washington | 69 |
| *UCLA 103 | California | 69 |
| *UCLA 107 | Stanford | 72 |
| *UCLA 73 | Southern California | 62 |
| *UCLA 91 | Brigham Young | 73 |
| *UCLA 57 | Long Beach St. | 55 |
| *UCLA 68 | Kansas | 60 |
| *UCLA 68 | Villanova | 62 |
| UCLA 109 | Washington | 70 |
| UCLA 100 | Washington | 83 |
| UCLA 85 | Washington | 55 |
| UCLA 92 | Oregon | 70 |
| UCLA 91 | Oregon St. | 72 |
| UCLA 85 | California | 71 |
| UCLA 102 | Stanford | 73 |
| UCLA 79 | Southern California | 66 |
| UCLA 90 | Weber St. | 58 |
| UCLA 73 | Long Beach St. | 57 |
| UCLA 96 | Louisville | 77 |
| UCLA 81 | Florida St. | 76 |

## 1971–72

| UCLA 105 | The Citadel | 49 |
|---|---|---|
| UCLA 106 | Iowa | 72 |
| UCLA 110 | Iowa St. | 81 |
| UCLA 117 | Texas A. and M. | 53 |
| UCLA 114 | Notre Dame | 56 |
| UCLA 119 | T.C.U. | 81 |
| UCLA 115 | Texas | 65 |
| UCLA 79 | Ohio St. | 53 |
| UCLA 78 | Oregon St. | 72 |
| UCLA 93 | Oregon | 68 |
| UCLA 118 | Stanford | 79 |
| UCLA 82 | California | 43 |
| UCLA 92 | Santa Clara | 57 |
| UCLA 108 | Denver | 61 |
| UCLA 92 | Chicago Loyola | 64 |

## 1972–75

| UCLA 94 | Wisconsin | 53 |
|---|---|---|
| UCLA 73 | Bradley | 38 |
| UCLA 81 | Pacific | 48 |
| UCLA 98 | Santa Barbara | 67 |
| UCLA 89 | Pittsburgh | 73 |
| UCLA 82 | Notre Dame | 56 |
| UCLA 85 | Drake | 72 |
| UCLA 72 | Illinois | 64 |
| UCLA 64 | Oregon | 38 |
| UCLA 87 | Oregon St. | 61 |
| UCLA 82 | Stanford | 67 |
| UCLA 69 | California | 50 |
| UCLA 92 | San Francisco | 64 |
| UCLA 101 | Providence | 77 |
| UCLA 87 | Chicago Loyola | 73 |
| UCLA 82 | Notre Dame | 63 |
| UCLA 79 | Southern California | 56 |
| UCLA 84 | Washington St. | 50 |
| UCLA 76 | Washington | 67 |
| UCLA 93 | Washington | 62 |
| UCLA 96 | Washington St. | 64 |
| UCLA 72 | Oregon | 61 |
| UCLA 73 | Oregon St. | 67 |
| UCLA 90 | California | 65 |
| UCLA 51 | Stanford | 45 |
| UCLA 76 | Southern California | 56 |
| UCLA 98 | Arizona St. | 81 |
| UCLA 54 | San Francisco | 39 |
| UCLA 70 | Indiana | 59 |
| UCLA 87 | Memphis St. | 66 |

## 1973–74

| UCLA 101 | Arkansas | 79 |
|---|---|---|
| UCLA 65 | Maryland | 64 |
| UCLA 77 | Southern Methodist | 60 |
| UCLA 84 | North Carolina St. | 66 |
| UCLA 110 | Ohio U. | 63 |
| UCLA 111 | St. Bonaventure | 59 |
| UCLA 86 | Wyoming | 58 |
| UCLA 90 | Michigan | 70 |
| UCLA 100 | Washington | 48 |
| UCLA 55 | Washington St. | 45 |
| *UCLA 92 | California | 56 |
| *UCLA 66 | Stanford | 52 |
| *UCLA 68 | Iowa | 44 |

*ULTIMATE WINNER: Bill Walton's teams were known for their winning streaks.*

and two NCAA championship series—during Bill's first two seasons. But the final year provided an even more difficult early season schedule. Yet despite the appearance of Maryland and North Carolina on the slate, he continued to pace the team to victory game after game. Then after 10 of those victories his troublesome back began to pain him too much, and he had to sit out three contests while the Bruins awaited their important match with Notre Dame. When Walton came back, the victory streak was stopped at 88 in the historic game against Notre Dame at South Bend.

But Walton had taken part in 70 of those triumphs, plus 20 straight as a freshman and 49 straight in high school.

Though his personal statistics with the UCLA varsity—633, 612, and 522 points in successive years for an average of just about 20 points a game—will not stand out in history, his feat of playing for teams that won 139 straight games may stand up forever.

# Coach Lost Only
# 10 Games in 10 Years

When coach W. J. Wisdom picked up a book on basketball at the campus book store of Tarleton State Junior College in the late 1920s, he was taking the first step toward making a bit of basketball history.

Tarleton wasn't a basketball-minded school at the time, which was typical of football-conscious Texas. Wisdom, in fact, was a football coach first—and a pretty good one. His teams compiled a 68–28–12 record.

But basketball turned out to be Wisdom's specialty. Though he had never played the game himself, the coach lost only 10 games in ten years in the 1930s. He taught one-handed shots and full-court presses long before they became common strategies.

Stressing fundamentals, Tarleton's Texans had only two plays. But that didn't keep the scores down. During its 86-game winning streak between 1933 and 1938, Tarleton won by such scores as 92–17, 72–6, 77–11, and 63–4. When competition at the junior-college level was hard to find, Tarleton took on four-year institutions. (Today, Tarleton itself is a four-year school.)

The winning streak was ended in 1938. But before long, the coach was putting together another skein of 25 games.

Not until UCLA ran up 88 victories had a college team topped Tarleton State.

Among college basketball's other outstanding streaks is the 129 in a row the University of Kentucky won at home through 1955. That home-court dominance had begun in 1943.

The San Francisco University teams that featured Bill Russell ran up a 60-game winning streak even though the school did not have a gym of its own.

# Basketball's Winningest Coach

High-school basketball had its Prof. Ernest Blood, college basketball its John Wooden, and pro basketball its Red Auerbach—winners all. But for pure success, year in and year out, no coach ever matched the triumphs of Bob Douglas.

Douglas was part owner and coach of an all-black touring team called the Renaissance. Unlike the Harlem Globetrotters, the "Rens" took their basketball seriously, playing as many as 140 games a year against the best available competition of their era. From 1922 through 1948, the Rens took on such teams as the Original Celtics (featuring Joe Lapchick, Nat Holman and others) and the rest of the best professional outfits, black or white.

The Rens established an all-time pro record in 1932–33 when they ran up 88 straight victories, including several against the Celtics. That season, the Rens trimmed the Celtics in seven of eight meetings.

The mastermind of the Rens' success had to be Douglas, a dapper-looking man who was a native of the West Indies. Douglas had learned the game of basketball in 1909. He joined the Rens in 1922 when they were playing games in ballrooms and improvised gyms throughout the United States. Basketball was just beginning its growth at the time. One thing America wasn't about to tolerate then was integrated teams. That enabled Douglas to assemble some of the greatest black stars.

The first team he put together won 38 games and lost 10. They continued to tour and meet all comers in an era when there were no formally organized professional leagues. But people began noticing the all-black quintet when it split six games with the supposedly invincible Celtics in 1926–27. After that, the Rens were a must team for any tournament calling itself a world's professional championship.

The Rens peaked in the 1932–33 season with their 88-game streak. They defeated the Globetrotters, who were playing serious basketball at the time, in a tournament billed as the world championship in 1939. The Rens also won a half-dozen other high-caliber pro tournaments before Douglas stepped down in 1948.

When the coach's record was totaled, it showed a whopping 2318 victories against only 381 defeats. That's more than twice as many as Red Auerbach, whose triumphs are outstanding in their own right.

*STAR OF STARS: Hardly a season went by in his career that Oscar Robertson did not make some All-Star team.*

# All-Star All the Time

For a player on a team that doesn't win a championship, any post-season glory can only come from the fellow players, media people and others who select all-star teams. Oscar Robertson is certainly one of the truly great players of all time—an all-star in every sense of the word. But for most of his career, his college and professional teams were out of the running for championship trophies.

"The Big O" did not lack, however, for all-star mentions. As a junior and senior at Crispus Attucks High School in Indianapolis, Oscar made high-school All-America two times, which is a rare feat in itself. He then went on to star at the University of Cincinnati. As a freshman he was not eligible to play for the varsity. But once he donned a Bearcat uniform, he was an instant success.

Sophomore Robertson averaged 35.1 points a game to lead the country in scoring. He was named consensus All-America (the first five) by the National Collegiate Athletic Association.

As a junior and senior, Oscar averaged 32.6 and 33.7 to again lead the nation in scoring. Naturally he was also a consensus All-America again. But being listed as one of the top five college players should not be taken for granted. Only a few other collegians (Jerry Lucas, Pete Maravich, Lew Alcindor, and Bill Walton among them) have achieved this honor. And only Tom Gola did it before Oscar came along.

But unlike his championship days at Crispus Attucks, Robertson could not bring home a winner. Not that he didn't try. The Bearcats got into 10 NCAA post-season games while he was on campus and finished in third place twice. For the 10 games, he averaged 32.4 points. In one game, he set a record with 56.

As a pro rookie in the 1960–61 season, Oscar was an immediate success. He averaged over 30 points a game for the Cincinnati Royals and swept the All-NBA and Rookie of the Year honors.

For nine more years in a row, Oscar was first-team All-NBA. Once, in the 1963–64 season, he was the runaway choice for Most Valuable Player honors.

Never before had a player been so consistently honored, year after year, at the high school, college and professional level. For 14 straight seasons, he was voted the best there was at the level of competition he was playing. No other player can make that claim.

And yet he did it with teams that did not come very close to winning championships.

Along with his all-league honors in the pros, Robertson got into the limelight at midseason All-Star games often. He made the best of these outings, scoring over 20 points in eight of the first ten All-Star games he played in and 17 and 18 points in the others. He has averaged over 20 points in the midseason classics.

# Three Average 20 Points and 20 Rebounds in Season

In the history of professional basketball, only two big men have ever accomplished the rugged double of averaging over 20 points and 20 rebounds in a season. Wilt Chamberlain, naturally, was one—and he did it often. Bob Pettit, a lanky 6-foot-9 former forward, was the other, while he was playing with the old St. Louis Hawks.

Plus one little man.

Jerry Lucas once made the comment that he was 6-foot-7¼ inches tall as a high-school sophomore and that he never grew a fraction of an inch after that. In college he was often listed as 6-8 and in the early years as a pro, 6-9.

If publicists were prone to overstate Lucas' height, it was perhaps because he "played taller."

Lucas was always a great technician on the basketball court. His shooting percentages both from the floor and free-throw line were excellent and his passing game was superb. Thus it should come as no surprise that he could burrow his way under the backboards and scoop out rebounds despite his lack of size. He did it with timing and quick hands.

In 1965–66, while playing for the old Cincinnati Royals, Jerry performed the rare feat of combining his scoring and rebounding to the degree where he averaged over 20 in each department.

In 79 games that season—his third in the league—Lucas totaled 1668 rebounds for an average of 21.1 a game. As a scorer he averaged 21.5 points.

And for good measurement, he also topped 20 in each department in the playoffs.

*WHEN HISTORY BEGAN: With just 3 seconds on the clock at Munich, West Germany, a long night was still ahead for the U.S. Olympic team in 1972.*

# Who Should Have Won Olympics in 1972?

It was September 9, 1972, in the midst of a troubled Olympics at Munich, West Germany. If medals were awarded for turmoil, the 1972 Games would have been the all-time lock for a gold, with athletes dying at the whims of terrorists, with boxers being jobbed by officials, with an athlete having his gold medal taken away for "illegal" drug use because he used a pill to curb his asthma.

If anything seemed predictable at Munich, it would have been that the United States would beat the U.S.S.R. in the final game of the basketball tournament, extend its winning streak to 64 games going back to 1936, and go home with its eighth straight gold medal. The U.S. had not lost an Olympic men's game before that night. And for anyone who saw the game in person, at the Olympic arena Basketballhalle, or on worldwide television, there was a feeling the U.S. should not have lost, either.

Yet the final score was U.S.S.R. 51, U.S. 50.

Kevin Joyce, a co-captain of the American team from the University of South Carolina, was one of the key players in the tournament, and particularly at the end of the game. Joyce echoed the feelings of many when he recalled years later: "I thought we would definitely win. I didn't think we had a chance to lose. It's not that we took the Russians lightly. But we were so far ahead of everybody."

But even Joyce admitted that after the first half, when the U.S.S.R. jumped to a 26–21 lead, "I might have underestimated them."

The Russians were no slouches. On their 12-man roster were players who had a cumulative 1,881 international games, played under different rules than the

*COMING BACK: Even before the controversy started at Munich, the U.S. needed a comeback before its final-seconds showdown with the U.S.S.R. Bobby Jones (No. 5) is shooting for the Americans in the second half.*

Americans, mostly collegians, were used to. The U.S. players had 51, with more than half of those by a player who didn't figure in the final game. But the Americans had a strong team, built around Jim Brewer of Minnesota, Mike Bantom of St. Joseph's, James Forbes of Texas-El Paso, Tom McMillen of Maryland and Dwight Jones of Houston up front, and Doug Collins of Illinois State, Tom Henderson of Hawaii, Ed Ratleff of Long Beach State and Joyce to move the ball.

Still, the Russians, led by Sergei Belov, kept the U.S. at bay. When the Americans closed the gap, the Russians would widen it, until they built a margin of 8 points with 6:07 to play.

As the Russians worked at running out the clock, the American coach, Hank Iba, junked his sluggish game plan and turned to a fast-break, pressing style that probably better suited the American team.

Joyce, Forbes and McMillen came into the game. Henderson stole a pass and Forbes tipped in a shot to make the score, 44–38, in favor of the U.S.S.R. Joyce caught fire, making three baskets and an assist in two minutes time to pull the U.S. within 3, and Collins made two free throws to cut the lead to 47–46. The Soviets, meanwhile, were held without a basket for seven minutes coming down the stretch.

Down by 3 with 36 seconds left. Forbes popped a jumper and finally, with 3 seconds left, Collins went to the free-throw line for two shots that could put the U.S. into its first lead of the game. The Russians led, 49–48, but Collins had been deadly on his earlier four foul shots.

What happened after that would make this game the most infamous in basketball history.

Collins made his first shot to tie the game. The official quickly grabbed the ball and returned it to Collins for his second shot, thus putting the ball in play, according to international rules, and thus ruling out a possible timeout. But the buzzer sounded for a timeout. It was ignored by the officials, and Collins promptly made his second shot, giving the U.S. a 50–49 lead.

There were three seconds to play as Belov took the ball downcourt. But confusion reigned. With two seconds gone, an official called a timeout to clear up a mess that was developing with Russian coaches storming the scorer's bench and fans moving down on the court.

The clock was reset to three seconds, after the intervention—completely beyond the rules—of R. William Jones, a Briton who headed the international basketball federation. Before the clock was reset, however, a Russian took a desperation shot and missed. The U.S. players hugged each other in ecstasy.

But the celebration was short-lived. Jones, again illegally overruling the game officials, insisted that there was an error and ordered the clock reset again at 3 seconds.

The befuddled Americans took the court as the Russians took the ball out at the far end of floor for one more desperation try. This time, 6-foot-8 Alexander Belov stationed himself under his basket, with the 6-foot-9 Forbes to his side and Joyce not far behind in the backcourt.

More confusion with rules. McMillen, at 6-foot-11, was waving his stork-like hands to harass the inbound passer when an official told him to move back. Though McMillen was within his rights, he did. Belov, meanwhile, had spent more than the allotted 3 seconds in his keyhole, contrary to international rules. As a long pass sailed to Belov, he gave Forbes a sharp elbow, an obvious foul, and Joyce overshot Belov as the ball was coming to him.

Belov made the basket, putting the Russians ahead to stay, 51–50, as time ran out.

"It was the first time in any sport where both teams had the feeling of winning in the same game," lamented Joyce. "Only minutes earlier, we were rejoicing and had the feeling of winning and they were down in defeat. Then it reversed."

In the U.S. locker room, the Americans decided not to accept silver medals. But that was minute, compared with the other activity going on. The American officials protested, but one member of the five-man international basketball committee had already left the arena. An official appeal was made, but Jones's committee was made up of three Communist-bloc members and two from the Western World. The appeal was overruled, 3–2.

This was despite the fact that the referee and the timekeeper verified the illegalities in sworn statements. All documentation showed that Jones acted illegally, but months later another appeal to the International Olympic Committee was turned down, too.

When Joyce was asked what he thought Jones had on his mind by his actions, Joyce recalled: "Maybe he was trying to change basketball. Maybe he did. You can see changes in international basketball. It's more balanced now."

But for Joyce and his teammates, there was only second place and unwanted medals. The silver medals are still in a vault in Munich. A few years ago, the Munich Olympic Committee made one more try to see if the American players still wanted them. No one accepted. The team has never met for a reunion, unlike many U.S. teams. The players are still bitter.

Joyce, however, is proud of being part of that team and wears his Olympic ring as well as a necklace his mother made with the Olympic symbol dangling from it.

Appropriately, the necklace is gold, not silver.

*AGELESS: Bob Cousy put on his sneakers to play an NBA game when he was 43.*

# • V •

# Odds and Ends

## Age Gaps in the NBA

The oldest player? Coach Bob Cousy, the longtime Boston Celtic hero, was perturbed with his Cincinnati Royals team's inability to bring the ball down court during the 1969–70 season. So he donned a uniform himself to show them how. Cousy wasn't the playmaker of old, so he gave up after seven games. However, he was an old playmaker—43 years old to be exact.

Not to diminish Cousy's 7-game effort, but the oldest regular in NBA history was Kareem Abdul-Jabbar, who played the last game of his 20-year career on June 13, 1989, just short of two months after his 42nd birthday.

Jabbar played 74 regular-season games that year, plus 15 more in the playoffs.

With each game played, Jabbar was making history at the end of his career. He finished with many of the most important career NBA records, including most seasons played (20), most games played (1,560 in the regular season) and most minutes played (57,446 in the regular season). He scored the most points (38,387 for a 24.6 average in regular season), plus numerous other marks. In the playoffs, he set career records for games played (237), most points (5,762 for a 24.3 average) and many other categories. He helped take teams to the playoffs in 18 of his 20 seasons. He also participated in 19 All-Star games, the last of which was after his 42nd birthday.

*TEENAGE PRODIGY: Bill Willoughby made it to the NBA at age 18.*

For years, the youngest player in the NBA's history was Joe Graboski, who was three months shy of his 19th birthday when he joined the Chicago Stags in 1948 right out of high school.

But in 1975, after the earlier success high school player Moses Malone had in going right to the NBA, the league's teams began a more serious scouting of schoolboys.

In that year's draft, two teams—the Philadelphia 76ers and the Atlanta Hawks—took high school players within the first two rounds. The 76ers got a 19-year-old named Darryl Dawkins out of Orlando, Florida. The Hawks made Bill (Poodle) Willoughby of Englewood, New Jersey, their second-round pick.

Willoughby made his NBA debut with the Hawks on October 23, 1975. At the time, he was 18 years, 5 months, 3 days old. Though he never was a star, he did last a decade in the league with several teams.

# The Referee Who Worked Overtimes

When Max Tabacchi blew his whistle to begin a National Basketball Association game between the old Rochester (N.Y.) Royals and the Indianapolis Olympians on January 6, 1951, he didn't know what he was getting in for. The game was played at Rochester, which usually meant an easy victory for the home team. In fact, during a two-season span, the Royals were 62–6 on their floor at 5,000-seat Edgerton Sports Arena.

The Olympians, a talented team that included five players from one of the great University of Kentucky quintets, decided that the best way to defeat the Royals in Rochester was to play a tight ball-control game. There was no 24-second clock back in the pros at the time, and to win with the Royal wizards Red Holzman and Bob Wanzer performing their deft ball-handling was next to impossible.

So Tabacchi and his fellow whistle-tooter, Sid Borgia, had a very easy time for four quarters. Neither team went for the basket much. The Olympians held the lead after the first period, even though they had scored only 20 points.

The game remained tight for the first three periods. Then, in the final quarter, the ball-control antics got simply ridiculous. However, the Royals put on a stretch drive near the end of regulation play, to tie the score at 65–65 and put the game into overtime.

It was then that history began to be made.

The teams continued their deliberate style of play, which emphasized a tight grip on the ball. The crowd of 3,300 fans ho-hummed through the first five-minute overtime, as each team scored two points. The second overtime was even drearier with neither team scoring. In the third period, each team got a basket and that was it. In the fourth overtime, neither scored. Thus in four overtime periods, the two professional teams had combined to score eight points in 20 minutes of play.

The fifth overtime, with the clock approaching midnight, brought action by both teams to end the fiasco. But when the Olympians and Royals ended that period, the game was still tied—now at 73-all.

The Royals began to revert back to drab ball-control play in the sixth overtime, hoping to take the perfect shot. They held the ball for 3½ minutes. After a time out, however, the Olympians forced the Royals into a situation where one player had to take a desperation shot. The Royal missed and Indianapolis' great Alex Groza, an ex-Kentuckian, grabbed the rebound and passed it down floor. Paul Walther relayed it to Ralph Beard, another ex-Kentucky superstar, who was near the foul line. Beard dribbled once and then arched a looping shot through the hoop. Only one second remained on the clock at the time. The ball game was finally over, after a record 78 minutes.

Holzman, who later coached the New York Knicks to their greatest moments, has commented that a six-overtime game is a thing of the past now that the 24-second rule is in effect. It was instituted three years after that game.

"I doubt that it will ever happen again," said Holzman, who played 76 minutes that night. "The 24-second clock forces a team to shoot. And don't forget the shooters are great today. It's very tough for two teams to keep trying in overtime periods. Something's got to give."

But referee Max Tabacchi had not seen the last of basketball marathons. About two years later he was officiating a college game in Albany, N.Y., between Niagara University and local Siena College. The date was February 21, 1953. The game started at 9:15 P.M.—the second

## ROCHESTER VS. INDIANAPOLIS
### FOR 76 MINUTES
#### Rochester

| | FGA | FGM | FTA | FTM | Reb. | Ast. | PF | Pts. |
|---|---|---|---|---|---|---|---|---|
| Wm. Calhoun | 11 | 6 | 1 | 0 | 3 | 0 | 1 | 12 |
| J. Coleman | 14 | 7 | 2 | 1 | 9 | 4 | 2 | 15 |
| R. Davies | | | | did not play | | | | |
| Wm. Holtzman | 9 | 1 | 1 | 1 | 2 | 7 | 0 | 3 |
| A. Johnson | 6 | 0 | 1 | 1 | 5 | 1 | 1 | 1 |
| J. McNamee | 3 | 2 | 0 | 0 | 1 | 0 | 0 | 4 |
| P. Noel | | | | did not play | | | | |
| A. Risen | 27 | 11 | 6 | 4 | 8 | 1 | 3 | 26 |
| F. Saul | 9 | 3 | 0 | 0 | 5 | 0 | 2 | 6 |
| R. Wanzer | 6 | 3 | 1 | 0 | 1 | 0 | 0 | 6 |
| Totals | 85 | 33 | 12 | 7 | 34 | 13 | 9 | 73 |

#### Indianapolis

| | FGA | FGM | FTA | FTM | Reb. | A st. | PF | Pts. |
|---|---|---|---|---|---|---|---|---|
| C. Barker | 0 | 0 | 0 | 0 | 2 | 2 | 0 | 0 |
| L. Barnhorst | 7 | 4 | 1 | 1 | 2 | 5 | 3 | 9 |
| R. Beard | 23 | 8 | 1 | 1 | 5 | 1 | 1 | 17 |
| Alex Groza | 12 | 8 | 1 | 1 | 4 | 0 | 0 | 17 |
| J. Holland | 3 | 0 | 0 | 0 | 1 | 0 | 0 | 0 |
| "Wah Wah" Jones | | | | did not play | | | | |
| R. Lavoy | 13 | 6 | 1 | 1 | 2 | 0 | 3 | 13 |
| M. McMullan | 8 | 2 | 3 | 3 | 3 | 4 | 2 | 7 |
| P. Walther | 15 | 4 | 4 | 4 | 3 | 3 | 1 | 12 |
| Totals | 81 | 32 | 11 | 11 | 22 | 15 | 10 | 75 |

#### Score by Periods

| | 1 | 2 | 3 | 4 OT | 5 OT | 6 OT | OT | OT | Total |
|---|---|---|---|---|---|---|---|---|---|
| Rochester | 10 | 23 | 20 | 12 | 2 | 0 | 2 | 0 | 4 | 0 | 73 |
| Indianapolis | 20 | 18 | 19 | 8 | 2 | 0 | 2 | 0 | 4 | 2 | 75 |

half of a doubleheader. Niagara had a powerful team and Siena a mediocre one, just trying to post a .500 record as the season drew to a close.

It was a surprisingly nip-and-tuck game, with Siena making a brave attempt to upset the tournament-bound Niagara team. At the end of regulation play, the Siena team had matched Niagara's score. Then a Niagara player took a long one-hander from a sidecourt that went in. However, the timer, from Siena, ruled the basket was too late. Niagara argued—for a full ten minutes—but to no avail. An overtime was set.

The score at the end of regulation play was 54–54, which was below average for the times, but not far below.

In the first overtime, the teams went at it pretty heavily. They tied each other 7–7. The next overtime was more cat-and-mouse, each team looking for the good shots, which never came. Each team scored two points.

Then in the third extra stanza, they broke loose. But again they knotted the score. And again in the next overtime they tied.

Finally, in the sixth overtime, with players from both teams hit hard by fouls (Niagara lost five players), the game was broken open. Larry Costello got hot and tallied six points before fouling out in the last 20 seconds. Eddie Fleming, Niagara's other pro-bound star, held the team together.

At 12:17 A.M., more than three hours after the tipoff, the two teams closed out 70 grueling minutes of basketball with Niagara on top, 88–81.

Fleming, who played all 70 minutes, changed his jersey number to 70 for the rest of his career. Costello, who played 69 minutes, became No. 69.

# At 5-feet-9, an All-America Center

The list of players under 6 feet who have made consensus All-America since 1950, is appropriately, short. The NCAA Guide names only five. Anyone who has such stature needs extra-special skills, but none of the five stood out like Johnny O'Brien of Seattle University. He was a 5-9 center.

Forget his height—O'Brien stood tall among basketball's best in the early 1950's. As a junior in 1951–52, he became the first collegian to score more than 1,000 points (1,051) in a season. He also made 361 free throws that year, another record. Because several of his games were not against four-year institutions, his point total did not count as an NCAA record, but in his senior year he set the official mark with 884, and he finished with 2,537, also the record. His averages in his final two years were 28.4 and 28.5. In 1953, he set some NCAA tournament records, including most points in three games (97) and most free throws in a game (18).

When the Associated Press announced its All-American Team in 1953, Seattle's Mighty Mite was the second-biggest vote-getter, ahead of future Hall of Famers Tom Gola of La Salle and Bob Pettit of LSU and well ahead of a couple of other scoring machines, Frank Selvy of Furman and Bevo Francis of Rio Grande. Only 6-11 Walter Dukes of Seton Hall got more votes.

Those who saw O'Brien play were amazed. Seattle played the Harlem Globetrotters in an Olympic fund-raising game during Johnny's junior year, and it was a close contest that forced the Trotters into a straight game. O'Brien scored 43 as the Chieftains stunned the Trotters, 84–81, prompting the Trotters' legendary center, Goose Tatum, to say: "That O'Brien ain't no little man. He's a giant."

How Johnny O'Brien of South Amboy, N.J., got to play center is almost as amazing as how he got to Seattle U.

First things first.

Johnny and his twin brother Eddie, also 5-9, had a tough time making the South Amboy St. Mary's High team. Johnny got to start as a junior and Eddie as a senior. They were better baseball prospects, but their father wanted them to try college first. But Johnny insisted that anyone who took him would have to take Eddie, too, and the college insisted that they couldn't chance taking two 5-9 players. So the twins sat out a year.

Then in 1949 they went to a semipro baseball tournament in Wichita, Kansas, as members of a South Amboy team. One of their games was against a Mt. Vernon, Wash., team, whose first baseman was Al Brightman, the baseball and basketball coach at Seattle. The coach knew of the O'Briens through an old Eastern friend.

In the first inning against Mt. Vernon, Johnny drew a walk and Brightman began making one of the most improbable recruiting pitches in history. When Johnny reached base, the coach began asking him if he would be interested in Seattle, what were his grades, and so on. Johnny told the coach to also talk to his brother, and sure enough, Eddie was soon on base.

Johnny later recalled the game. "We had a lot of time to talk," he said, "because the game went 17 or 19 innings."

Johnny's bid for a package deal worked, and the twins enrolled at Seattle in the fall.

As freshmen, both played guard—and played well. But it wasn't until their sophomore year that Johnny moved to center.

"It was during our third or fourth game, and we were behind, 23–21, at the half," said Johnny. "Coach Brightman was mad when he came into the locker room and told me: 'You go in at center. I'll give you five minutes to do something.' He meant it. Well, we outscored the other team, 59–20, and won."

Johnny remained in the pivot on offense after that. With Eddie feeding him, he blended his array of left- and right-handed hooks and push shots, jumpers and two-handers with uncanny leaping ability to awe—and beat—opponents. He would start the game at guard, move into the center on offense, then move out on defense, replaced by the Chieftains' tallest starter, 6-3½ Wayne Sanford.

Johnny recalled that his success had partly to do with the way teams played then. "They were stationary, and we confused them with our quickness. They played a lot of zones, and that would open it up for us. Brightman always said the best defense was a good offense."

Johnny liked to "keep them guessing" and would use different shots the first three times down the court— usually a series consisting of a left hook, a right hook and a jumper.

He was dangerous because he was accurate and also drew fouls. Against rival Gonzaga in one game, he made 17 of 21 from the floor and 17 of 19 from the line.

O'Brien was not just setting personal records, however. Crowds increased tenfold in his four years at Seattle, and he helped turn the Chieftains into a winner. Johnny led them in the NCAA tourney as a senior, which was the beginning of the end to his basketball career.

In his first NCAA game, an 88–77 victory over Idaho State, Johnny scored 42 points, 2 short of the tourney record. Then came a showdown with powerful Washington. Time ran out on the dream machine as Johnny got only 24 but the Huskie All-America center, Hooks Houbregs, set a tourney record with 45, and Washington won, 90–72.

Johnny laughed about that game.

"Funny thing is," he said, "that was the one game in my career where we thought about defense, and it got us in trouble. We had a scheme to stop him and 'held' him to 45."

That was a Friday night. On Saturday, Johnny bowed out of college basketball with a 30-point effort as Seattle beat Wyoming in a consolation game. On Sunday, the twins signed with baseball's Pittsburgh Pirates and on Monday they were on their way to spring training in Havana, Cuba.

Johnny, like Eddie, lasted a few years in the majors, as an infielder and pitcher. Then he returned to Seattle, where he became operations manager of the Kingdome.

What, he was asked, would happen if he now told someone in a bar he was once an All-America center? "I wouldn't say that," he answered.

"What if you were with me and I told somebody that," he was asked.

"They'd probably say we both had too much to drink."

# Shoots Fouls from His Knees

As a youth growing up in West Virginia, Rod Hundley was beset with personal problems. To escape his woes, Hundley turned more and more to the basketball court, which became his second home.

But the pressures of basketball affected him, too, so Hundley devised a few antics to help him let off steam. By the time he enrolled at the University of West Virginia, he had become "Hot Rod" Hundley.

Hot Rod scored well for the Mountaineers. And consistently, too—750 points as a sophomore, 711 as a junior, 798 as a senior.

But there were times when his shots weren't as consistent in form as they were in their completion. The most famous was his "Praying Mantis" in which he went to his knees at the foul line to sink a free throw against the University of Pittsburgh. Under more crucial conditions, with West Virginia meeting George Washington University for its conference championship, Hundley went to the foul line in overtime—and hooked a free throw!

# "Good Old Doug," All-America at 31

When the basketball players at St. Mary's University in San Antonio, Texas, referred to one of their teammates as "Good Old Doug," they meant *old*.

Doug Williams was a pretty fine player growing up in Phoenix City, Ala., back in the 1950s. But he forewent his college education for a six-year stint with the United States Air Force. Later he was recalled to duty in Korea, too.

But the 6-foot-9 father of four maintained his basketball interest as he neared 30 years of age. While still in his late 20's, he entered St. Mary's University. There he scored 511 points as a freshman. He even got better as a sophomore, with 643 points, and blossomed as a 30-year old junior with 605.

Williams' scoring slipped in his senior year (to 487) but not because of advancing age (basketball-wise). Actually, Williams was becoming a more polished player and tending to the rebounding chores for a good small-college team. His coach said he could have averaged 30 points if he wanted to during his final season, 1969–70. But Williams blended in nicely with St. Mary's controlled-style basketball.

"He's the fellow who keeps the other players cool," said coach Ed Messbarger.

How he kept his cool was amazing. His daily schedule during basketball season went like this: classes in the morning, a quick lunch and a short study session, a two-hour stint as an employee of the school, practice, pick up the kids, eat supper and study. Since his wife worked, sometimes he had to prepare dinner.

"At times, I'm so tired that I just sit and stare at the book and it stares back at me." he said.

The people who select all-America teams, however, aren't concerned with one's non-sports routine. So in 1970, when Williams was named a first-team "All" selection by the National Association of Intercollegiate Athletics (NAIA), he knew it was solely for his basketball ability—of which he still had a lot.

# Touches Basket Rim with His Foot

Valery Brumel got his place in sports history for his heroics in the high jump. The Russian athlete, who won the 1964 Olympics and set numerous jumping records, is considered by most authorities as the best man ever at that event. Astonishingly, Brumel could jump more than 16 inches over his own height. He also could long jump over 25 feet.

Americans, who were used to dominating the high-jump event, had trouble believing Brumel's feats when he emerged as a standout at the 1960 Olympics. He was only 18 at the time, but he upset America's strong favorite John Thomas at the Rome Games and nearly won the gold medal. After those Games, the sports world was curious about Brumel's development.

Russia wasn't as open to the Western World in 1961 as it is now. Only bits and dribbles of sports information leaked out of the Soviet Union.

But the Americans who had doubted Brumel's ability were astounded to see a legitimate photograph taken of him in '61. The photo, which was circulated to dispel any doubts, showed Valery Brumel touching the rim of a basket in a Russian gymnasium—*with his foot.*

Brumel had actually leaped so high that he made contact with the rim with the inside of his lead foot. The Russians did not bother to explain the circumstances that prompted the photograph, but then maybe they didn't have to. The 6-foot-1 Brumel's "feet" spoke for itself.

Another high-jumping basketball exploit was done often by one of the touring Harlem Globetrotters, basketball's comics.

In one of their more serious moments, the Trotters

would place a quarter on top of the backboard, about 12 feet off the ground. Then Jimmy Jackson, their best leaper though far from their tallest player, would pick the quarter off the board.

# Small Court, Big Scoring

The Lithuanian Club of Shamokin Pa., "held" Pee Wee Kirkland to 47 points, causing his scoring average to drop drastically. A 47-point game makes a dent when your average is 70.

But in mid-January, 1974, the 27-year-old Kirkland got untracked and scored 135 points against the same Lithuanian semi-pro quintet for the finest night of his career. Pee Wee—whose real first name is Rich—uncorked 62 field goals and canned 11 of 19 free throws. It was his second 100-point game of the season.

Pee Wee, a 6-foot-2 ex-New Yorker, also had had games of 60, 79, and 82 points.

His team, the Hilltoppers, averaged over 160 a game.

Pee Wee and the Hilltoppers had to credit much of their success to the fact that they only played at home. Their smallish 82 × 40-foot gym was conducive to scoring, and their vocal partisan crowd made some opposing team uncomfortable.

Pee Wee played for the Federal Penitentiary team in Lewisburg, Pa.

# He Scored 25 Points
# Without a Single Field Goal

During the early part of the 1970–71 college basketball season, Florence State University of Alabama pinned a pretty good 89–61 defeat on its cross-state rival, Birmingham Southern College. So Southern's Panthers decided to change their strategy for the return match on January 30, 1971. They went to a ball-control style of play.

The Panthers carried their strategy to the extreme, trying for only 8 field-goals (and making 5 of them). At the half, they led, 21–18. Meanwhile, Florence State shot 24 times, making 17. But the Birmingham Southern strategy won out. The Panthers won the game, 54–46.

Slowdown games produce few individual stars, particularly for the team that holds the ball. But the Panthers had a clear-cut hero that night. He was the team captain, Russell Thompson.

A guard, Thompson controlled the ball—and the strategy—for his team. He followed his coach's orders perfectly, not shooting once from the floor. But that didn't hurt his scoring average a bit. In a game in which he didn't have a single field-goal attempt Russell Thompson scored a total of 25 points!

As he held the ball away from the Florence team, Thompson was fouled often. He went to the free-throw line for 28 shots—and made 25 of them. Meanwhile, five Florence players left the game on fouls trying to wrest the ball away.

For the season, Thompson was a dead-eye foul shooter, making 84 per cent of his tries.

## U.S in the Olympics
## THE 63-GAME WINNING STREAK
### (F indicates final game)

| Score | Margin | Leading U.S. Scorer/Points |
|---|---|---|
| *1936 at Berlin* | | |
| U.S. 2, Spain 0 (forfeit) | — | None |
| U.S. 52, Estonia 28 | 24 | Frank Lubin 13 |
| U.S. 56, Philippines 23 | 33 | Joe Fortenberry 21 |
| U.S. 25, Mexico 10 | 15 | Samuel Balter 10 |
| U.S. 19, Canada 8 (F) | 11 | Fortenberry 8 |
| | | |
| *1948 at London* | | |
| U.S. 86, Switzerland 21 | 65 | Alex Groza 19 |
| U.S. 53, Czechoslovakia 28 | 25 | Vince Boryla 9 |
| U.S. 59, Argentina 57 | 2 | Gordon Carpenter, Don Barksdale 12 |
| U.S. 66, Egypt 28 | 38 | Barksdale 17 |
| U.S. 61, Peru 33 | 28 | W. "Wah Wah" Jones 12 |
| U.S. 63, Uruguay 28 | 35 | Bob Kurland 19 |
| U.S. 71, Mexico 40 | 31 | Groza 19 |
| U.S. 65, France 21 (F) | 44 | Groza 11 |
| | | |
| *1952 at Helsinki* | | |
| U.S. 66, Hungary 48 | 18 | Dan Pippen 15 |
| U.S. 72, Czechoslovakia 47 | 25 | Bob Kurland 12 |
| U.S. 57, Uruguay 44 | 13 | Kurland 21 |
| U.S. 86, U.S.S.R. 58 | 28 | Kurland 15 |
| U.S. 103, Chile 55 | 48 | Clyde Lovelette 25 |
| U.S. 57, Brazil 53 | 4 | Lovelette 11 |
| U.S. 85, Argentina 76 | 9 | Lovelette 25 |
| U.S. 36, U.S.S.R. 25 (F) | 11 | Lovelette 9 |
| | | |
| *1956 at Melbourne* | | |
| U.S. 98, Japan 40 | 58 | Bill Russell 20 |
| U.S. 101, Thailand 29 | 72 | Ronald Tomsic 15 |
| U.S. 121, Philippines 53 | 68 | Bob Jeangerard 21 |
| U.S. 85, Bulgaria 44 | 41 | Jeangerard 19 |
| U.S. 113, Brazil 51 | 62 | Russell 17 |
| U.S. 85, U.S.S.R. 55 | 30 | Russell 20 |
| U.S. 101, Uruguay 38 | 63 | Tomsic 18 |
| U.S. 89, U.S.S.R. 55 (F) | 34 | Jeangerard 16 |
| | | |
| *1960 at Rome* | | |
| U.S. 88, Italy 54 | 34 | Adrian Smith 17 |
| U.S. 125, Japan 66 | 59 | Jerry Lucas 28 |
| U.S. 107, Hungary 63 | 44 | Oscar Robertson 22 |
| U.S. 104, Yugoslavia | 42 | Robertson, Terry Dischinger 16 |
| U.S. 108, Uruguay 50 | 58 | Smith 15 |
| U.S. 81, U.S.S.R. 57 | 24 | Jerry West 19 |
| U.S. 112, Italy 81 | 31 | Lucas 26 |
| U.S. 90, Brazil 63 (F) | 27 | Lucas 23 |

*1964 at Tokyo*

| | | |
|---|---|---|
| U.S. 78, Australia 45 | 33 | Jerry Shipp 16 |
| U.S. 77, Finland 51 | 26 | Shipp 18 |
| U.S. 60, Peru 45 | 15 | Shipp 18 |
| U.S. 83, Uruguay 28 | 55 | Joe Caldwell 16 |
| U.S. 69, Yugoslavia 61 | 8 | Shipp 22 |
| U.S. 86, Brazil 53 | 33 | Lucius Jackson 17 |
| U.S. 116, Korea 50 | 66 | Jim Barnes 26 |
| U.S. 62, Puerto Rico 42 | 20 | Bill Bradley, Shipp 16 |
| U.S. 73, U.S.S.R. 59 (F) | 14 | Jackson 17 |

*1968 at Mexico City*

| | | |
|---|---|---|
| U.S. 81, Spain 46 | 35 | Spencer Haywood 12 |
| U.S. 93, Senegal 36 | 57 | Haywood 16 |
| U.S. 96, Phililppines 75 | 21 | Bill Hosket 16 |
| U.S. 95, Panama 60 | 25 | Haywood 27 |
| U.S. 100, Italy 61 | 39 | Haywood 26 |
| U.S. 73, Yugoslavia 58 | 25 | Jo Jo White 24 |
| U.S. 61, Puerto Rico 56 | 5 | Haywood 21 |
| U.S. 75, Brazil 63 | 12 | White 14 |
| U.S. 65, Yugoslavia 50 (F) | 15 | Haywood 21 |

*1972 at Munich*

| | | |
|---|---|---|
| U.S. 66, Czechoslovakia 35 | 31 | Tom Henderson 16 |
| U.S. 81, Australia 55 | 26 | Ed Ratleff 16 |
| U.S. 67, Cuba 48 | 19 | Dwight Jones 18 |
| U.S. 61, Brazil 54 | 7 | Henderson 12 |
| U.S. 96, Egypt 31 | 65 | Mike Bantom 17 |
| U.S. 72, Spain 56 | 16 | Bantom 11 |
| U.S. 99, Japan 33 | 66 | Bantom 18 |
| U.S. 68, Italy 38 | 30 | Jim Forbes 14 |
| U.S.S.R. 51, U.S. 50 (F) | −1 | Henderson, Jim Brewer 9 |

# INDEX